W9-AWB-739

SATCHEL PAIGE

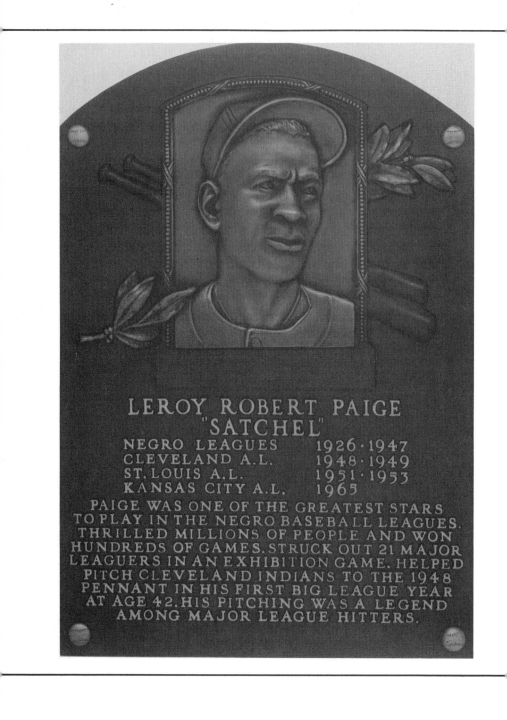

LEROY ROBERT PAIGE
"SATCHEL"
NEGRO LEAGUES   1926·1947
CLEVELAND A.L.   1948·1949
ST. LOUIS A.L.   1951·1953
KANSAS CITY A.L.   1965
PAIGE WAS ONE OF THE GREATEST STARS
TO PLAY IN THE NEGRO BASEBALL LEAGUES.
THRILLED MILLIONS OF PEOPLE AND WON
HUNDREDS OF GAMES. STRUCK OUT 21 MAJOR
LEAGUERS IN AN EXHIBITION GAME. HELPED
PITCH CLEVELAND INDIANS TO THE 1948
PENNANT IN HIS FIRST BIG LEAGUE YEAR
AT AGE 42. HIS PITCHING WAS A LEGEND
AMONG MAJOR LEAGUE HITTERS.

ADAIRE SCHOOL LIBRARY

SATCHEL PAIGE

by Kathryn Long Humphrey

An Impact Biography
FRANKLIN WATTS
New York London Sydney Toronto
1988

12,918

Photographs courtesy of: National Baseball Hall of
Fame and Museum, Inc., Cooperstown, N.Y.: cover, pp.
2, 29, 58; Brown Brothers: pp. 26, 64; The Granger
Collection: p. 46; UPI/Bettmann Newsphotos: pp. 47, 71,
95; The Bettmann Archive, Inc. p. 73; AP/Wide World
Photos: pp. 79, 85; National Baseball League: p. 89.

Library of Congress Cataloging in Publication Data

Humphrey, Kathryn Long.
Satchel Paige.

(An Impact biography)
Bibliography: p.
Includes index.
Summary: Surveys the life and career of the Negro
League's pitching phenomenon, the first baseball
player in the Negro Leagues to be inducted in the
National Baseball Hall of Fame.
1. Paige, Leroy, 1906–1982   —Juvenile literature.
2. Baseball players—United States—Biography—Juvenile
literature. 3. Pitching (Baseball)—Juvenile
literature. 4. Negro American League—Juvenile
literature. [1. Paige, Leroy, 1906–1982. 2. Baseball
players. 3. Afro-Americans—Biography] I. Title.
GV865.P3H86 1988 796.357'092'4 [B] [92] 87-25304
ISBN 0-531-10513-X

Copyright © 1988 by Kathryn Long Humphrey
All rights reserved
Printed in the United States of America
6 5 4 3

CONTENTS

SATCHEL PAIGE

For my parents,
George and Ellen Long,
Mr. and Mrs. Baseball
of Eastern Iowa

With special thanks to:
Cool Papa Bell
Bob Feller
William Guilfoile
Ed Hamman
Babe Herman
Judy Johnson
Buck Leonard
Joe McGuff

1
DOWN BY
THE BAY

Leroy Paige ran toward the passengers getting off the train at the Mobile, Alabama station. "Need your bags toted, sir?" he asked a man who towered over him. The man looked at Leroy's ragged clothes and turned away.

"Ma'am, can I help you with your satchels?" Leroy asked a woman whose wrinkled face looked bone tired.

He could earn a nickel or a dime for every bag he carried, and he needed the money. Leroy had just figured out a way to rig a pole and some ropes together to carry several satchels at once, and he expected to earn a lot. The woman sighed and nodded toward a big green suitcase. As the train puffed away, Leroy struggled to carry the suitcase and three satchels with his new invention.

"You look like a walking satchel tree!" a friend shouted.

The other boys agreed. Soon everyone was calling Leroy "Satchel." And "Satchel" Paige he remained for the rest of his life.

Leroy "Satchel" Paige was born in Mobile, Alabama in the early nineteen hundreds. The exact date has been debated for years. A birth certificate in the Mobile courthouse shows Leroy "Page" with a birthdate of July 7, 1906. Because the last name is not spelled "Paige," some people are suspicious of this date, but it has been accepted as his official birth date. Satchel used to say his birth record was lost because the family goat ate the Bible with the date written in it. When reporters questioned his mother, she said, "What mother knows when her child is born?"

Leroy's parents, Lula and John Paige, already had six children when Leroy was born. Four more came later. All thirteen of them lived on South Franklin Street in a four-room house that was one long row of rooms. To provide for the large family, John worked as a gardener, and Lula was a washerwoman.

Yet the Paiges had barely enough money for food, and none for luxuries such as toys. Satchel often entertained himself by throwing rocks, and he developed a good aim. Whenever his mother sent him to bring a chicken from the chicken coop, he killed it with a rock. He and the other boys made a game of knocking cans off tree stumps with rocks. When they were sweaty from playing, they ran to the bay to wash off. They were careful where they went along the shore, though. Blacks were not allowed on certain sections of the beach.

When Leroy was six his mother enrolled him in the W.H. Council School, a school for black children, but Satchel did not attend very often. The first few times he skipped school, his mother scolded him, but she finally gave up. Besides, she wasn't so sure book learning was all that useful.

What she cared about was whether he earned money to bring home for food. With her large family, Lula had to ladle out the food carefully so it would go around. Any money Leroy could add to the grocery budget was welcome. When he was very small, Leroy collected empty bottles and sold them. But when he was seven, his mother thought he was ready for a real job. She heard that some neighbor kids were toting bags at Union Station, so she sent Leroy to work with them.

Leroy, or Satchel, as he came to be called, worked hard during his childhood, but he found time for trouble, too. Whenever he went to his school, he passed by a white school. And there was always a gang of white kids waiting to fight with Satchel and his schoolmates. Satchel used his good aim with rocks and hit a lot of boys. Often, he was beaten up in return, and sometimes he got into trouble with the police. His mother was always furious with him. Satchel wondered if she understood what it felt like to be called "dirty nigger" and to be treated like he had some kind of disease because he was black.

When Satchel was ten, he heard Coach Wilbur Hines at the W.H. Council School announce baseball tryouts and Satchel decided it would be fun to throw something besides rocks. He was picked for the team to play first base and outfield.

Then, during a game in the middle of the season, the team's two pitchers gave up six runs in the first inning. Although Satchel was one of the youngest players, Hines had noticed how well he threw and called him in to pitch. Satchel was so tall and skinny that when he stood on the mound, all anyone could see were arms and legs. He whizzed the ball past the first three batters he faced and struck them out. By the end of the game, he had struck out sixteen batters and had not given up a single hit.

After the game, Hines told Satchel that he would be the team's number one pitcher. Although Satchel became known for his pitching around the south end of Mobile, he was still kind of a loner.

John Paige was glad his son was playing baseball. He asked him if he wanted to be a baseball player instead of a gardener when he grew up, and seemed pleased when Satchel said yes. He couldn't buy any baseball equipment, though. The family was just too poor.

They were so poor that at twelve Satchel had never owned a baseball or a new toy. One day as Satchel walked by a toy store in his tattered clothes, he had a strong desire to have some of the toys. Even though he had no money, he went into the store. When he thought no one was looking, he slipped a handful of toy rings in his pocket.

Before he got out the door, a man yelled at him and asked him what he was doing. The next thing Satchel knew he was being taken to the police station. He waited there as the police called to ask his mom to come to the station. The police also talked to the truant officer, and she told them about the rock throwing and gang fights and skipping school. Satchel had a feeling he was in more trouble than he had ever been in before.

But when everyone finished talking, they let Satchel go home for the night and told him to see the truant officer in the morning. His mother was crying hard when they left the police station, but she didn't yell at him when they got home. She was still crying when Satchel went to bed.

His mother didn't say much in the morning. The two of them just got ready and left. The truant officer talked for a long time. Satchel did not understand much of what the woman was saying, and he was eager for the talk to be over so he could get out of there. He promised himself he was not going to fight that day. And he would work especially hard at the railroad depot so he could bring home extra money. Then the truant officer stood up and said that Satchel would be committed to the Industrial School for Negro Children at Mt. Meigs.

Satchel had never thought taking the rings would lead to reform school. He would be taken away from everything and everyone he knew. He was so upset he couldn't think.

2
FROM MT. MEIGS
TO BIRMINGHAM

The drive to Mt. Meigs took less than an hour. Then the door locked behind Satchel at the reform school, which would be his home for the next five and a half years. He felt sick inside. He was taken to a dormitory. He didn't have clothes to hang on the wall pegs, except the ones given to him at Mt. Meigs, usually called the Mount.

The staff at the Mount wanted to help the boys find constructive ways to use their time. They made lists of what the boys liked to do, and tried to get them involved in activities such as woodworking, drawing, music, and sports. After he had been there a week, Satchel tried out for baseball. "Let's see how you throw," the coach said when Satchel told him he was a pitcher.

Satchel went to the mound and took a quick warm-up and started throwing. No one could hit his pitches. When the coach called Satchel over, he was smiling. "That arm might do you some good some day," he said. "Put all that . . . feeling you put in throwing rocks into throwing baseballs, and you might make something of yourself."

Satchel thought a lot about what the coach said and wondered if he could earn a living playing baseball. He began to realize that his talent was something special, and he made up his mind to work hard to develop it. The coach showed him how to put up his foot and how to swing his arm around. Satchel was so tall and thin—and his feet were so big—that when he wound up, the kids couldn't tell where the ball was. But they did know there was not much chance of getting a hit when Satchel pitched.

The coach taught him that by watching their knees he could tell where the batters' weaknesses were. He practiced for hours at a time, developing his control. Month after month, Satchel worked on his game.

But he did other things besides pitch. For one thing he went to school regularly. At the Mount there was no skipping. And he liked music. When baseball season was over, he spent a lot of time singing. He became a choir leader and played the drum in the drum-and-bugle corps.

Though he'd been afraid and lonely when he arrived, Satchel later looked back on his days at Mt. Meigs as a positive influence on his life because he got away from the street gangs in Mobile. He said if he had stayed there he might have grown up to be a crook like some of the people he ran around with. At the Mount he had regular meals, a warm place to sleep, and a chance to develop his pitching.

In 1923 Satchel was discharged from the reform school. By then he had grown into a skinny six-foot-three-and-a-half-inch seventeen year old. When he arrived home that day, his brothers and sisters were there to celebrate—and he was happy to see them all again. Although he had been gone a long time, the house seemed the same as always.

His mother gave him a month to take it easy and get used to life in Mobile again. Then she sat him down and told him it was time to start helping out the family.

Satchel walked all over town looking for a job, but people who knew he had been at Mt. Meigs were afraid to hire him. He wondered what kind of future he would have with his reform-school record. One day after job-hunting he went to Eureka Gardens where his brother, Wilson, pitched and caught for the Mobile Tigers, an all-black semipro team. Satchel sat in the stands and watched the Tigers work out. When a kid came up and asked to try out for a pitching position, the manager sent him to the mound to pitch and then hit every pitch the kid threw.

Satchel knew he could throw a lot better than that. When the kid left, Satchel walked up to the manager and asked if he still needed a pitcher. At first, the manager told him to go home. He had seen enough amateurs. But when Satchel said he was Wilson's brother, the manager gave him a chance. Satchel fired ten balls. He threw so fast and hard that the manager couldn't hit one of them.

"Do you do that constantly?" the manager asked.

"No sir," Satchel said. "I do it all the time."

The manager laughed. "If you want the job, you've got it. We don't charge admission so your pay will depend on the collection at the game. If we take in enough, we'll give you a dollar a game. When the collection ain't so good we can give you a jug of lemonade."

Satchel was excited about the chance to play semipro baseball. But when he told his mother about it, she was upset and said it wasn't any kind of work for a man. She thought Satchel and Wilson should not be wasting their time playing baseball.

Satchel tried to explain that playing for the Tigers would help them earn a reputation and maybe some day they would be picked up by one of the teams up North. Black teams couldn't play against white teams in the South, but they could in the North. And some of the players earned a lot of money.

But his mother was firm. She was a religious woman, and she thought it was sinful for grown men to play base-ball. She especially hated Sunday baseball games. She told him to find a real job. Satchel pleaded with her to try to understand. He said he would keep looking for another job, but he wanted her to understand that he loved baseball more than anything in the world. His mother just shook her head and told him she would never watch him play baseball.

Satchel's mother had been deeply hurt when Satchel was sent to the reform school. He didn't want to hurt her again. He thought about what he should do, and changed his mind half a dozen times. But baseball was really his love, and even at that time he had some sense of his pitching genius and felt compelled to develop it to its fullest. He finally decided to join the team.

Besides the pitching, he found a regular job sweeping up at the Mobile Bears' stadium. The Bears were a white minor-league team. Some of the Bears' players heard what a great player Satchel was and asked him for a demonstration. After they saw his speed and control, one of them said, "Too bad you aren't white." Over the next forty years, Satchel would hear that same comment many times.

He immediately became the star player of the Mobile Tigers. He threw the ball so fast it looked like a pea when it crossed the plate. And he could throw it exactly where he wanted to. The fans were awed by his control, and he began to call attention to it. He sometimes ignored the regular home plate. He would place a gum wrapper on top of it and tell everybody that the gum wrapper was his home plate. Then he would hurl the ball right over the wrapper. The fans roared. They loved his showmanship, and he loved the attention he got from them.

But the fans could be demanding. In a game played after he had pitched twenty-six straight wins, Satchel had a one to nothing lead and two outs in the ninth inning. Then his teammates made three straight errors, and their opponents loaded the bases. People all over the ballpark started booing.

Satchel was amazed at how quickly the fans switched from cheers to boos, and he was angry. He motioned for his outfielders to sit down on the grass. They thought he was crazy and yelled in protest. But Satchel insisted and finally got them to sit down. Then he turned to pitch to the next batter—with no outfielders.

The crowd stopped booing and stared at Satchel. He fired. Strike one! The crowd cheered. He threw the next ball. Another strike. The whole crowd stood up. Finally strike three, and the crowd went wild. The cheering went on long after the game ended, and stories about this tall, skinny pitcher began to spread.

In 1924, Satchel won thirty games for the Tigers. For the next couple of years he played for the Tigers as well as other semipro teams in the area.

In 1926 Satchel's friend, Alex Herman, offered him a job with the Chattanooga Black Lookouts for fifty dollars a month. He was thrilled, but later he said, "To tell the truth, I would have played for nothing. That's how much I loved baseball." The Lookouts were in the Southern Negro League, and although they were a weak team, it would be a step up for Satchel to be part of the league at all. Coach Herman also wanted his brother Wilson, but Wilson didn't want to leave Mobile.

Herman insisted on getting permission from Satchel's mother before taking Satchel with him. Lula Paige protested. Satchel's father had died less than a year before, and she did not like the idea of Satchel going away so soon after his death. Besides, she never had liked baseball.

Herman told her that with the money Satchel earned he could help out more with the family bills and promised that he would mail the money to her himself. With that, Lula Paige softened and finally agreed to let Satchel go.

In Chattanooga, Satchel stayed in a rundown boarding house for two dollars a week. It was the first time he had ever had a room to himself. He didn't have many clothes to hang in the closet there.

Herman had recognized Satchel's extraordinary talent and pushed Satchel hard to develop his pitching. He would point to a small hole in the fence and say, "Throw through that hole until you can get it through every time. Then try knocking down those bottles I lined up at home plate."

Satchel was determined to perfect his game. He practiced before the other players were up in the morning, and he stayed at it long after they went home at night. The practice paid off. The control that Satchel would become so famous for improved steadily.

After playing a few home games in Chattanooga, the Lookouts were ready for a road trip. Satchel could not believe how rundown the team bus was. Riding on dirt roads full of potholes to Memphis, Tennessee was extremely uncomfortable. When they arrived at the ballpark about nine o'clock at night, Satchel decided not to get off the bus.

"The bus is leaving," Herman told him.

"Just have the driver take me to the hotel or wherever we're staying."

"*This* is where we're staying," the coach said. And Satchel spent the night sleeping on his suitcase at the ballpark. It was the first time but it would not be the last. His back ached, and his mouth was full of dust. For breakfast he ate a hot dog and washed it down with a bottle of lukewarm soda. And the ball field with its rocks provided poor playing conditions the next day.

Satchel brought in crowds. After a month with the Lookouts Herman raised his salary to one hundred dollars, and Satchel couldn't wait to spend it. He bought new clothes and took his date out for a steak dinner. And he kept on spending. Before his next payday he had to ask Herman for an advance to pay his room rent.

Late in the season, Satchel left the Lookouts for a month to play for a New Orleans team, not so much for the eighty-five dollars they paid him, but because they gave him an old jalopy. Though Herman was angry about

Satchel going off like that, he took him back, and Satchel stayed with the team for another year. During his second year with the Lookouts, he traded in the jalopy for a flashy roadster. He loved the car so much that he was sometimes late for games because he was busy polishing it.

Satchel became a folk hero in the South. "Have you seen that Satchel?" fans would ask. They said Satchel should be playing for the majors, and Satchel also believed that he should. He was frustrated because—even though he had the talent—he was not allowed in the major leagues because of the color of his skin. Crowds poured into baseball parks to watch him. Would he pitch a shutout today? they wondered. Would he call the outfield in? They cheered and stomped when he threw the ball over a gum wrapper or a half dollar.

And though league players often played rough, Satchel did not. Several of the pitchers in the league threw at the batters, but Satchel refused to do that. "I don't call that no kind of baseball, if I have to cave their ribs in to get them out," he said.

In 1927, the manager of the Birmingham Black Barons, the best Negro league team in the South, asked Satchel to join his team. Satchel was more excited than he had ever been. He was steadily moving up in baseball and extending his reputation further and further. In his first game playing for the Barons, he struck out eighteen batters. Newt Allen, who played against him, said, "His arms were so long and he'd raise up that big foot, and the next thing you'd know, the ball was by ya."

Outfielder Jimmie Crutchfield, Satchel's teammate on the Barons, reported, "The only big thing we had was Satchel. When he was pitching, we'd have 8,000 people out there. And that was something for Birmingham."

Sportswriters said Paige could pitch right through a catcher's mitt. The fans had never seen such a fastball. They expected perfection. If Satchel let a player hit even one foul ball, some people would say he was having a bad day and would boo him.

Once when Satchel gave up a walk, and another batter got on base because of an error, his opponents laughed at him. "You're such a pop off," they said. "We were hoping you would get into a spot like this."

Satchel walked over to the other team's bench and told them he was going to strike out the next six batters. He retired the side with three strikeouts in a row. In the next inning Satchel struck out the first two batters, and grinned when his opponents made a white flag from a baseball shirt and waved it in surrender. The next batter popped up.

After the game his catcher ran to him. "How come you only struck out five when you promised six?"

"Aw, they had already surrendered," Satchel said.

Satchel continued in the Southern Negro League, pitching at least three or four times a week and getting twelve to twenty strikeouts a game. Sometimes he played in a doubleheader then drove two or three hundred miles on dusty roads to play in another doubleheader the next day.

Satchel filled the ballparks. The crowds wanted to see his superb pitching. And they wanted to see Satchel, the tall, skinny pitcher with the big feet and the unusual windup. Watching him on the field made people laugh, more with him than at him. Satchel liked the laughter and encouraged it. He had never rushed into a game. Because it amused the crowd, he began to emphasize his long slow walk to the mound, and it became a Satchel Paige trademark.

Satchel played all over the South. As he went from town to town, he was disturbed to find many places where blacks weren't welcome. "You can't stay in this hotel," he was told. "We don't serve colored here." Everywhere there were signs "Whites only" or "Colored," marking separate drinking fountains or separate entrances. "I sure don't know what we did to white folks to make them hate us so much," Satchel said in an interview with sportswriter Morris Henderson years later. He listed problems such as, "No place to sleep, beds in ditches, black cups, couldn't eat indoors."

These bothered him tremendously. But he seemed to forget whatever was bothering him when he put on his uniform and went onto the field. His uniform was like a magic suit. As Satchel once said, "(If) you love something the way I love baseball . . . ain't nothing going to bother you when you're playing." There were often some whites in the stands. A few of them called him "nigger," but most of them cheered.

In 1929 Satchel began playing winter ball in the West Indies and Latin America, something he would continue to do for nearly thirty years. The pay was always good, and it got him away from the prejudice in the United States for a while each year.

When he came back to the States in the spring of 1930, he played for the Elite Giants, first in Nashville, then, later in the year, in Cleveland. At the end of the regular season, Satchel wanted to keep playing baseball.

In those days, players from several major league clubs got together after the league season ended and formed a team which played all over the United States and Canada. Negro League players did the same. This practice of playing exhibition games around the country, especially in small towns and rural areas, was called barnstorming.

After the 1930 league season Satchel joined a barnstorming team called the Black Sox, which played some exhibition games against the Babe Ruth All-Stars, a team of major leaguers. Satchel never faced the legendary Babe Ruth in a game, because whenever Satchel was pitching, Ruth had a day off. However, he struck out such major league superstars as Hack Wilson and Babe Herman.

In one game against the Babe Ruth All-Stars in Los Angeles, Satchel struck out twenty-two major leaguers;

this beat the major league record for strikeouts. Fans crowded around him after the game, shook his hand, and congratulated him. They had never seen such a fastball.

The Elite Giants broke up before Satchel could begin his second season with them. In 1931 the United States was wallowing in the Depression, and it was a bad time to be out of work. But then Satchel received some good news. A Pittsburgh businessman, Gus Greenlee, was putting together a team that he called the Pittsburgh Crawfords. He intended to make the Crawfords the best team in Negro baseball, and he wanted Satchel to pitch. A chance to play on a top Northern team offered all kinds of possibilities. Maybe this was the break Satchel had hoped for since his early days with the Tigers?

3

____THE CRAWFORDS____

Except for a few players in the late eighteen hundreds, blacks had always been excluded from major league baseball. They played on all-black teams. The South had many black teams, but they were never allowed to play against white teams. This limited the size of the crowds and the amount of money Southern black players could earn. But in the North, blacks and whites played against each other in exhibition games after the major league season had finished.

Satchel was excited about playing for Gus Greenlee. Although the country was deep in the Depression, Greenlee had plenty of money from the numbers racket, and he put together a powerful team. He hired Satchel for $250 a month, which was a lot of money during the Depression. Gus had just the right catcher for Satchel. Many catchers had trouble holding onto Satchel's fastball. After bobbling a few of Satchel's throws, one catcher asked, "How's a guy supposed to catch Satchel Paige?"

"All a catcher has to know is when I'm throwing my

Satchel Paige was an early master of a variety of eccentric pitches including his jump ball, wobbly ball, blooper, drooper, and his famed hesitation pitch. Here, he reveals one of his particular grips on the ball.

bee ball and when I'm throwing my jump ball," Satchel said. "I throw both with the same overhand motion, only the bee ball goes off my fingers on the smooth hide and rolls level. My jump ball goes off the seams and jumps from four to six inches." Greenlee's catcher, Josh Rupert Gibson, was an outstanding hitter as well as a superb catcher.

In his first game for the Crawfords, Satchel was scheduled to pitch against the Homestead Grays, the top Negro League team. Greenlee wanted to test his new team against them. A huge crowd turned out for the game. Although Satchel's stomach churned, he was confident he could win. He was always at his best when a game was especially important. He struck out sixteen batters and beat the Grays.

After the game Gus Greenlee locked the door to the restaurant he owned, the Crawford Grill, and threw a private victory party. Gus announced that he was raising Satchel's salary to $700 a month and—as a bonus—promised to buy him two new suits.

People crowded around Satchel at the party, but Satchel noticed an attractive waitress and slipped away from the crowd to introduce himself. Janet Howard already knew who Satchel was. They spent most of the evening together, and when he took her home, he asked her for another date. There were many more to follow.

Gus brought in a lot of the big names in black baseball to play for the Crawfords, who became the most-feared team in the newly organized Negro National League. Many people believed that the Crawfords could have won a pennant in one of the white major leagues, and Satchel was given much of the credit. The *Pittsburgh Courier* carried statements such as, "(The) game was won by Gus Greenlee's blue-stockinged bunch . . . just another case of too much Satchel Paige on the mound." Or in another edition, "Satchel, elongated and a consummate showman, whose whipcorded right arm rifles a ball plateward with the speed of a bullet has as fast a ball as any ever uncorked in big league baseball."

Satchel was considered the number one player in Negro baseball and Josh was number two. One day Satchel and Josh were playing pepper, a warm-up game in which the ball is repeatedly thrown to a nearby batter who bunts it back to be fielded. "Someday we're gonna be playin' for different teams, and we're gonna have to face each other," Satchel said.

Josh swung his bat: "I'm in no rush for that."

"Yeah, but it's gonna happen," Satchel said. "I'll be pitchin' to you. You're the greatest hitter, and I'm the greatest pitcher, and we're gonna see who's best."

For the time being, however, the two players worked together and formed one of the best batteries in the history of baseball. When Greenlee promoted his Crawfords' games, he often advertised only Paige and Gibson, announcing: "Satchel Paige, guaranteed to strike out the first nine men, and Josh Gibson, guaranteed to hit two home runs." Other players on the team were jealous and thought they should get more recognition. But they could not deny that Satchel's pitching put money in their pockets because of the crowds that came to see him.

Gus Greenlee worried about the fans he had to turn away, and looked for a bigger ballpark. One day he told Satchel he had rented League Park, the Cleveland Indians' ball field, for a Crawfords' game. Plenty of fans came out, so Greenlee could afford the higher rent. After that, Gus began to rent other major league parks. Satchel couldn't help feeling proud that they had opened the major league parks to blacks so there would be room for the fans who wanted to see him do his stuff.

In addition to Satchel's blinding speed and pinpoint control, fans loved his antics. He had developed one of the most unusual windups in baseball. He cranked his arm around both ways half a dozen times, leaned way back, stuck his size fourteen foot in the air, and zoomed the ball by the batters.

When he joined the Crawfords he was already a hero

Satchel developed one of the most unusual pitching
styles in baseball. His tall, lanky figure and
size fourteen foot contributed to the peculiar
form of his famous windmill windup and delivery.

to blacks in the South. Now he gained recognition in the North and among whites. Everyone wanted to see Satchel Paige pitch. Everyone except his mother. She continued to believe that baseball was sinful. "I wish she'd change her mind," Satchel said. "It's a big strain when your mama ain't with you."

But the crowds were with him. Satchel always had a special communication with his fans. He was compared to Babe Ruth because of his skill and charisma. There was excitement when Satchel was in the game. With the Crawfords he had a winning streak of 21 straight games and 64 scoreless innings. If Janet Howard was in the stands, Satchel always put on a special show.

In addition to pitching for the Crawfords, Satchel often pitched in exhibition games against white teams at Yankee Stadium or other big league parks. Satchel's income grew. Besides sending money back to his family, Satchel bought Janet whatever she wanted and spent money on his clothes and hobbies. He had grown up without anything, but now he could afford luxuries. Gus Greenlee warned him to go easy on his spending, but Satchel believed that—with his pitching arm—he had nothing to worry about. He bought fishing equipment and several shotguns.

But he received the most publicity for the money he spent on cars. His fans called him car crazy. He constantly traded them. He ordered all the conveniences for his cars that could be found in the 1930s, such as reclining seats and loudspeakers for the radio.

Satchel took his car everywhere. In 1934 he drove all night to play in a doubleheader. At dawn he was so tired that he parked alongside a curb and slept in his car. That afternoon he pitched an extra-inning game. Things looked bad in the tenth. There were two men on base and no outs, and Satchel was about to face Buck Leonard, one of the greatest hitters in the Negro leagues. Satchel bore down and got Leonard out in three pitches. Then, with just six more pitches, he struck out the next two men. His team scored in the eleventh for a 2–1 victory.

"Satch wouldn't have let the game go that far," one of his fans told a reporter. "But he didn't have enough sleep. He could afford a hotel, but that car was brand new, and Satch lives with a new car like it was a bride."

Satchel did as he pleased much of the time. "He carried a boat on top of his car," Negro leaguer Judy (Julius) Johnson recalled. "If he saw a minnow jump up when he drove by a lake, he stopped the car and went fishing." Often he was more than half an hour late for a game. Or worse, he wouldn't make it at all. He would apologize and offer explanations: "I overslept." "I was fishing, and I plumb forgot about the game." "All the hotel clocks are wrong." "The taxi drivers are working for the other team." Other times he said that his car broke down and he had to stay and protect it.

The *Saturday Evening Post* reported that once he hit a dog on the way to a game. "I rushed him to the hospital," Satchel said. "And that poor thing looked like he was fixin' to die. It had me worried, so I stayed all afternoon, and I pulled that little dog through."

Another player might have been dropped from the team, but with Satchel, the manager just gritted his teeth and accepted Paige's excuses. When Satchel was pitching, the team won—and the gate receipts were good.

The fans, however, were not always so patient. Many came just to see Satchel and if he wasn't there they felt cheated. When he was late, chants of: "Where's Satchel? Where's Satchel?" filled the park. If he didn't show up at all, many demanded their money back.

Greenlee became a master at covering up for Satchel's absences, inventing stories of illness, injuries, car trouble, or whatever would work. In one small town where the crowd was especially restless, he stuck in a tall, lanky player and passed him off as Satchel. Amazingly, Greenlee got away with it.

4
MOVING WEST AND SOUTH

Satchel's girlfriend Janet was not happy about all the traveling Satchel had to do. She resented the time he was away from Pittsburgh. "When are we going to set a wedding date?" she asked after one of his trips.

"If you don't like it now when I'm gone," Satchel said, "what will it be like when we're married?"

"We'll manage," Janet said.

Satchel thought his traveling would cause even more trouble between them if they were married. "There'll be times when I'll be away for a long time."

Janet insisted they could work things out, and on October 26, 1934, they were married. Satchel had never managed his money well when he was single. After they were married, it was even harder to save money and he found himself broke most of the time.

"I'll see Gus," he said, "he'll give us more money."

But Gus Greenlee had financial problems of his own and refused. Satchel was angry. He thought about all the money his pitching had earned for Gus and decided to quit the Crawfords. He stormed out of Gus's office and went home to pack.

"Where are we going?" Janet asked. She didn't want to leave Pittsburgh.

"I don't know," was all Satchel could say.

It seemed crazy to quit a good job during the Depression. Millions of people were out of work and stood in soup lines to get something to eat. But Satchel was sure something would come along.

He was right. Within a few days, Neil Churchill, who owned a car agency, offered him a spot on his baseball club in Bismarck, North Dakota. Churchill was looking for an ace pitcher, and Abe Saperstein, Satchel's friend who owned the Harlem Globetrotters, had recommended him.

Although Satchel had never heard of Bismarck, and wasn't even sure it was in the United States, he agreed to take the job. For the first time he would be playing on a team with whites. Satchel and Janet headed for North Dakota and looked for housing. However, no one wanted to rent to blacks. Neil Churchill finally found a place for them, an old railroad freight car that had previously been used as a home for work gangs.

Janet complained that if they had stayed in Pittsburgh, they would not have to live in a place like that. But, though Satchel hated having to live in a boxcar, he argued that he had to have a job so they could eat.

At first Satchel faced discrimination on the ball field. The Bismarck players did not want a black on the team, but Satchel used his pitching ability to fight prejudice. To demonstrate his control, he put a small matchbox on a stick behind home plate and knocked it off thirteen out of twenty times. In his first game against Jamestown, a team that had regularly beaten and humiliated Bismarck, Satchel threw only his medium fastball and won. He pitched nearly every day. With Satchel on the mound, the team had an impressive record. In the end, his teammates were glad that Churchill had hired him.

After Satchel finished the regular season in Bismarck, he and Janet went to the Southwest for winter ball. Satchel formed a barnstorming team—the Satchel Paige All-Stars—that played in the California leagues. His favorite games of the winter season were those against Dizzy Dean's team of major league all-stars. Dizzy was a fastball pitcher like Satchel, and he dominated the major leagues at that time.

Pepper Martin, one of the best major league hitters, was on Dizzy's team. At one game Satchel asked every batter as he came up, "Are you Pepper Martin?" Finally, Pepper came to the plate. When Satchel asked if he was Pepper Martin, Pepper just grinned.

"They tell me you can hit," Satchel said. Pepper's grin broadened.

"Well, hit that!" Satchel said, and rifled the ball across the plate. Pepper swung and missed. Satchel struck him out in three pitches. The crowd buzzed with excitement.

Satchel was a perfect match for Dizzy. Young Bill Veeck, who would later play an important part in Satchel's career, sat in the stands of old Wrigley Field in Los Angeles for one of the most famous duels between Satchel and Dizzy. At the end of nine innings both teams were scoreless. "If you're not going to give us any runs," Satchel teased, "we're not going to give you any runs." Satchel's team finally scored in the thirteenth inning and won the game.

That season, Satchel and Dizzy Dean faced each other in six games, and Satchel won four of them. "You're a better pitcher than I ever hope to be," Dizzy told him. "If we played on the same team, we could take the league by the middle of the season and go fishing in the second half." Satchel was filled with pride at receiving such a compliment from the great Dizzy Dean. Later as people argued about who the country's best pitcher was, Dizzy said, "Let 'em argue. The best pitcher I ever seen is ol' Satchel Paige. My fastball looks like a change of pace alongside that li'l pistol bullet Satch shoots up to the plate."

34

While Satchel was enjoying great success in the West, the Crawfords had him banned from Negro baseball for jumping his contract, and the newspapers carried stories that Satchel would never again be allowed to play in the Negro leagues. The *Pittsburgh Courier* said, "The champ of today may be the chump of tomorrow." Satchel's stomach became queasy as he read the clippings.

The next summer Satchel returned to Bismarck. He led his team to their first national semipro championship and was named most valuable player. While he was in Bismarck, he met some Sioux Indians from a nearby reservation. There were snakes around the area, so his Sioux friends gave him an oil to use on snake bites. They warned him that it would burn when he put it on and that he should not use it unless he was bitten. But Satchel couldn't resist trying it on his pitching arm and rubbed on a generous amount. He liked it so much that he started using it regularly, but would never reveal the formula.

After the 1935 season, Satchel again went to the West Coast for winter ball. One of the most publicized games of that season took place in Oakland, California. Satchel's team played a major league all-star team that included Lou Gehrig. Their only nonmajor leaguer was a young player named Joe DiMaggio, who was scheduled to enter the majors as a New York Yankee the next season. Except for himself and his catcher, Ebel Brooks of the New York Yankee Black Sox, Satchel fielded a team of inexperienced players.

Young DiMaggio faced Satchel five times. He made three outs and was hit by the ball once, but in the tenth inning on his fifth trip to the plate, DiMaggio got a hit. Satchel smiled as he heard DiMaggio say after the game: "Now I know I can make it in the majors. I finally got a hit off Satch."

The major leaguers won the game, but Satchel's performance so impressed journalist Eddie Murphy that Murphy wrote in the *Oakland Journal*:

35

> The greatest pitching attraction in the world
> is being passed up by scouts, club owners, and
> managers only because the doors of organized
> baseball are closed to him.

Satchel appreciated the recognition. He was fully aware of his unique talent and knew that because of the color of his skin he might never get the full recognition he deserved. Later, in an interview with Morris Henderson of the *St. Louis Angus*, Satchel said, "If another man pitched like me and had been white, everything you picked up would have his name on it." Many sports editors said Satchel and other outstanding black players should be allowed in the major leagues.

Meanwhile, the Crawfords lifted their ban and invited Satchel to play for them in 1936. Janet had been complaining about living in the West for a year and a half, and so could not wait to get back to Pittsburgh. Satchel accepted the Crawfords' offer. He and Janet had planned to take a vacation before returning but they needed money, and Satchel canceled the vacation plans to accept an offer to pitch in Puerto Rico. Janet was angry.

When Satchel returned from Puerto Rico she was still angry. Janet wanted a husband who would come home every night, not one who was frequently in another city or country. Although they did not divorce for six more years, their marriage basically fell apart.

But Crawford fans weren't angry with Satchel. They came in droves to see him when he joined the team for the 1936 season. He drew record crowds throughout the summer. He also planned to play for the Crawfords the next year, but someone wanted to change his mind.

In the spring of 1937 Satchel was in New Orleans for spring training with the Crawfords. Scouts from the Dominican Republic, on the island of Hispaniola near Cuba, visited Satchel at his hotel and asked him to pitch for the Dominican Republic team.

At first Satchel refused, even though he was offered a lot of money. He had just gotten back on good terms with Gus Greenlee, and he didn't want to jump his contract again and spoil his standing with the Crawfords. The Dominicans raised their offer higher and higher. They spread huge sums of money on the bed in the hotel room and told Satchel to take what he wanted as an advance. Finally, Satchel weakened and agreed to play for them. Later, other Crawfords players also signed with the Dominican team.

Satchel and his friends were flown to the Dominican Republic, which was a big thing in those days. The people welcomed them as though they were royalty, and the team was taken to one of the presidential plantations for a picnic. At the picnic, a reporter warned Satchel that President Rafael Trujillo was so desperate for a winning team that the players might be killed if the team lost. "We didn't know it was a political thing down there," teammate "Cool Papa" Bell said.

Leaders in the Dominican Republic were in the middle of a feud. The Dominican people liked baseball, and President Trujillo was being challenged by opponents who fielded an excellent baseball team. Fans said they would support Trujillo if his team could win the baseball tournament.

Since winning could make the difference between whether he was president or not, Trujillo kept Satchel and his friends at a private club under armed guard. Everywhere the players went uniformed soldiers followed them. Satchel and his players also had to worry about Trujillo's political enemies who wanted them to lose. Whether they won or lost, they were in danger of being killed.

On the opening day of the tournament, the city was decorated with brightly colored flags, and huge crowds were on hand. Both Trujillo's armed guards and his opponent's armed guards came to the ballpark. Satchel was scared. He said later, "I knew whichever way the series went, I was lost."

37

The series did not go well for Satchel. His team, the Trujillo Stars, lost two games in a row, and Satchel's stomach bothered him a lot. President Trujillo was furious about the losses. When Satchel's team went back to their hotel after the second game, Trujillo's soldiers met them. "El Presidente doesn't lose," they shouted, and they fired their rifles into the air.

But the situation got even worse. The Trujillo Stars lost the third game. One more and the whole tournament would be lost. Satchel wondered about his chances of getting back to the States alive if they didn't win the tournament.

For the fourth game, Satchel's team bore down and played as well as they could, since it could have been the last game they ever played. They won, and then went on to win two more games to tie the series. The next game would decide who won the tournament.

On the day of the last game, Satchel went to the mound saying, "If we win, Trujillo's army is going to escort us off and protect us. If we lose there is nothing to do but consider ourselves passed over Jordan."

Satchel and his teammates put all their energy into that last game and won, giving the Trujillo Stars the victory for the tournament. Trujillo's army escorted them off the field as Satchel had said. Then Trujillo threw a big party for the team, even naming some of the food he served after the players. The next day the team flew back to the United States. Satchel never returned to the Dominican Republic.

5

THE MISERIES

Gus Greenlee was furious when some of his players went to the Dominican Republic, and he tried to get the State Department to do something about it. But by the time they returned, his anger was gone, and he was eager to have them play for the Crawfords again. The only penalty he imposed was a fine of one week's salary. However, Satchel and Gus couldn't agree on a salary. Gus offered $450 a month, but Satchel said he wouldn't even throw ice cubes for that pay and went back to barnstorming. Greenlee finally gave up on Satchel and sold his contract to Newark, but Satchel never played for the Newark team.

Satchel was at the peak of his career. Word of his pitching had traveled all over, and people throughout the country wanted to see the famous Satchel Paige. While many black players struggled to earn a living, Satchel was paid very well. He often made guest appearances and received as much as five hundred dollars to pitch only three innings. Once, he earned a thousand dollars—plus all expenses—to fly to Puerto Rico for a single game.

In October, after the major leaguers finished their season, he barnstormed against them with a team he organized and again called the Satchel Paige All-Stars. A sign on his Cadillac advertised, "Satchel Paige—Guaranteed to strike out the first nine men."

Now, instead of playing against the Dizzy Dean All-Stars, Satchel's most popular major league rivals were the Bob Feller All-Stars. "We had very good, close, one-run games," Feller said. In 1986, Feller rated Satchel as "probably as good as any pitcher today, and among the best pitchers of all time."

Describing how Satchel pitched, Feller said, "He could wind up like a windmill in a Kansas cyclone or he could throw the ball without a windup. He could throw from many angles, and he could throw change of speeds very well. He had four or five change-ups. His speed and control were excellent. His curve wasn't good, but it wasn't bad. When I first saw him, he had a little wrinkle of a curve."

Feller also remembered how tall and skinny Satchel was. "Satchel's legs were very thin. He used to wear three pairs of socks to make them look fatter."

For a while Satchel traveled with the bearded House of David team. Most of the players on the team belonged to the House of David religious order which believed that men should wear beards. The founder was an avid baseball fan and he established the baseball team which traveled from place to place. Although most of the players were followers of the religion, Satchel and some others were not. Satchel tried hard to grow a beard like the rest of the team, but all he could grow was a mustache. One day the other players presented him with a fake beard, and in the middle of a game, the whiskers got caught on his pitching arm and were yanked off. The crowd howled with laughter.

Satchel said that traveling around the way he did got in his blood, and when he was not on the road, he "had the misery" with him. He loved the crowds. He loved to perform. Fellow Negro League star, Julius (Judy) Johnson, said, "The bigger the crowd, the better Satch could pitch."

But pitching in a different town every day—sometimes two hundred miles from where he had been the day before—was physically wearing. As always, the crowd expected him to be perfect. If a batter even hit a foul off one of Satchel's pitches, the fans complained that Satchel was having an off-day and began to boo.

Late in the summer of 1938 as Satchel traveled across the United States playing baseball, he felt a lot of stress. His stomach began to bother him. Then when he went to pitch in the Mexican league, the spicy foods were hard on his stomach and made it feel worse. Soon the pain spread to other parts of his body and even his arm began to bother him.

When Satchel mentioned the arm problem, his manager suggested that he take a few days off. But Satchel had to keep pitching. He did not want to give up the paychecks or to disappoint his fans. He kept thinking he could work out the problem by throwing more often. He pitched four games in a row trying to work out the pain, but it got worse instead of better. Yet his pitching was still good, and his fastball was as fast as ever.

Then while playing in a game in Mexico City, his shoulder snapped so hard people around him heard the crack. Filled with pain, he dropped on the mound, unable to lift his arm. The manager rushed out to see what was wrong and took hold of Satchel's arm. Satchel screamed. As the manager helped him off the field, Satchel felt scared.

He rode back to the hotel and went to bed, hoping the rest would help him recover. He didn't want to believe that it was anything serious, but he awoke in the night feeling like a sledgehammer was pounding his arm and sending spasms of pain all over his body. He lay there praying that by some miracle the pain would go away and his arm would be normal again. But the pain did not disappear, and in the morning he still could not lift his arm.

The arm was so stiff that it was hard for him to put on his shirt. After he managed to dress, he left for the ballpark without bothering to put on his uniform. He went to the field and picked up a ball. His arm would not go up very far, but he threw the ball anyway. It rolled only a few feet.

Satchel went to see a doctor, but he could not help him. He visited other doctors in Mexico hoping for a cure, but could find none. Satchel returned to the United States and saw more doctors. Then he went to a specialist. The specialist examined him for a long time. Then the doctor told Satchel that he would probably never pitch again.

6

THE MONARCHS

Satchel was in shock. He had come a long way since those days of poverty in Mobile. He owned fancy cars and shotguns and clothes. And people looked up to him. But it was his arm that had gotten him where he was. If he couldn't pitch, what could he do?

Maybe he could coach. He called managers and asked for a coaching position. But they remembered the bad things. "You didn't show up for some of the games," they told him. "You didn't get to the park on time." Satchel wished he had been more careful. But when things had gone so well, he thought they would always be that way. Now he had no income and had to sell some of his shotguns to buy food.

When it was time for the winter meetings of the Negro League teams, Satchel felt discouraged about his future in baseball. With his bad arm and his reputation for jumping clubs, no one wanted to hire him, either as a player, a manager, or a coach. Then halfway through the season, Ralph Wilkinson, owner of the Kansas City Monarchs, called Satchel and told him he had bought his contract from Newark. Satchel had been depressed. Now he was excited again. He reported to Kansas City the next week and asked when he should join the Monarchs.

"You won't be playing with the regular Monarchs team," Wilkinson said. "We want you to go with our second team, a traveling team. You'll be going to the northwestern part of the United States and then heading up into Canada."

Satchel's excitement fizzled, but he was still glad to have a chance to play. "Why do you want me if I'm not good enough for the Monarchs themselves?" he asked.

"We think your name will still draw crowds," Wilkinson said. "And we thought you needed a hand."

Satchel was grateful to the Monarchs. He did draw crowds. And his arm improved so that he could throw the ball well enough to play first base or to bloop pitches toward homeplate.

But he knew his teammates were not happy to have a pitcher without an arm along. He forced himself to go to the ballpark day after day. People came to the games, curious to see a once-famous pitcher, but not expecting much from Satchel now. As he glanced at the quiet fans sitting in the grandstands, he thought back on the roaring crowds, who were awed by his pitching. Even the boos in past days were better than the quiet politeness of these fans.

At one game he heard a kid say, "I wonder how he ever got anybody out." The words stung. Satchel became so discouraged he didn't know what to do and even thought about quitting.

But Knut Joseph, his manager, was confident that Satchel would make a comeback. "Go throw the ball some," he would say. "Maybe you can work your arm back into shape."

Satchel pitched one or two innings at a time then went back to the hotel and soaked his arm in water that was so hot it nearly scalded him. He worried constantly, and his stomach bothered him. Then, after months of struggle, he went to warm up for a game after being out of the lineup for a few days. He threw to the catcher. Something was very strange. Satchel felt a lightness in his arms, and did not feel any pain. He threw again. Still no pain. He felt a glimmer of hope.

"I'm going to throw a fastball," he told the catcher.

The catcher looked at him as if he was crazy, but Satchel fired, then hummed one to the catcher. He had his old speed again. And the soreness in his arm had gone as mysteriously as it had come. Satchel jumped around the mound yelling, "My arm is back. I can pitch!"

Everyone in the park stopped what he was doing and watched as Satchel threw one fastball after another. He finished the warm-up and ran back to the dugout telling everyone how good his arm felt. Fans came to the game that day expecting a lackluster performance and were thrilled by Satchel's pitching. People who had never seen him pitch with a good arm were amazed. Satchel was overjoyed. He was making a new start. That night Satchel and Knut, his manager, called Wilkinson and told him the news.

"Work yourself back into shape real easy," Wilkinson said. "Then come and join us for the 1939 season."

Reporters asked Satchel what had made his arm improve, but he could not explain it. It was almost like a miracle. His pitching career, which looked like it had ended, was back.

In the summer of 1939, Satchel played for the Monarch's A team and became their ace pitcher. He went on to help them win the Negro American League title in 1939, 1940, and 1941. In addition to playing for the Monarchs, he made guest appearances for other teams.

In the 1941 Negro League East-West game, Satchel was saved for the final innings. The first batter he faced in the seventh inning was Lennie Pearson, an excellent

Satchel's success with various teams of the Negro Southern League led him to his starting position with the Kansas City Monarchs in 1939. Opposite: Satchel beams a triumphant smile after the Kansas City Monarchs win their third straight Negro American League title in 1941 with Satchel as the team's ace pitcher.

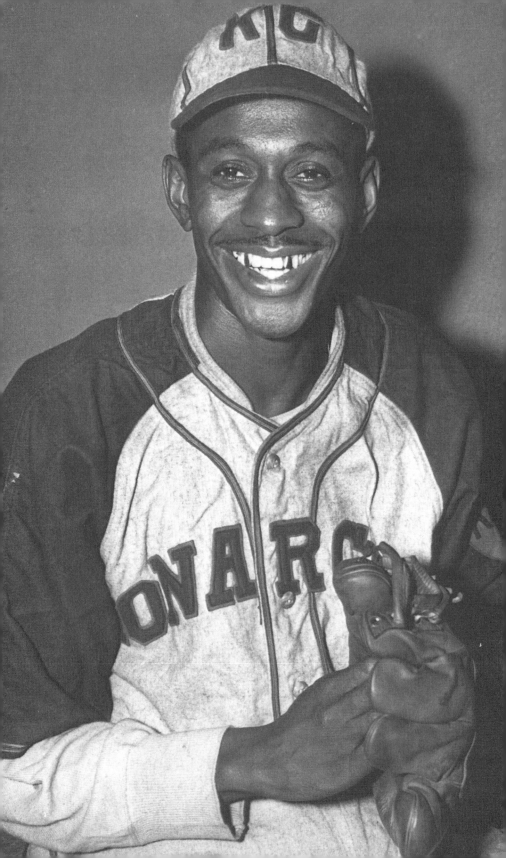

hitter. Monte Irvin, another good hitter, was on deck. Satchel struck out Pearson with three pitches.

"What's he throwing today?" Irvin asked.

"I don't know," Pearson answered. "I didn't see it."

Players reported that Satchel threw a small ball because he threw so fast it was hard to see the ball. Many called it a pea ball, because it seemed to get smaller as it approached the plate. Satchel often referred to his fastball as a bee ball because it hummed. Even if a player knew the kind of pitch Satchel was throwing, he usually couldn't hit it. There were so many stories about Satchel, it is hard to know which were true. One of the Paige legends said that Satchet wrote "FASTBALL" in large letters on the bottom of his long left shoe.

Satchel continued to play with the Monarchs. The problems he had faced when his arm went bad taught him to be more careful about honoring his contracts. He appreciated the help Wilkinson had given him when he needed it, and he intended to treat him fairly. In the 1940s Satchel was the main attraction for the Monarchs and they became the Negro League's best team. Their biggest challengers were the Homestead Grays of Pittsburgh on which catcher Josh Gibson, Satchel's former Crawfords' teammate, played. Josh was having his usual great season.

In July, 1942, Satchel faced the Grays at Forbes Field in Pittsburgh. Satchel felt especially in control that day, and he was eager to have a showdown with Josh. Before the game Satchel bet Josh that he could strike him out. Stringbean Satchel teased the Grays throughout the game. In the late innings, Satchel had not yet struck Josh out. With two out in the seventh, and two batters due up before Josh, Satchel decided to walk the two players ahead of him so that he could pitch to Josh. He told the catcher to step out so that he could throw four balls.

Buck O'Neil ran out to the mound from first base and asked Satchel what he was doing. He reminded him that if Josh got a hit, they could lose the game. Satchel smiled and told O'Neil not to worry. He walked the first batter. As Buck Leonard came to the plate Satchel called to Josh: "I'm going to put Buck on and pitch to you."

Josh grunted. When Josh came to the plate, a hush fell over the crowd. Satchel said, "Now I'm going to throw you a fastball." Josh swung and missed.

Then Satchel yelled, "Now I'm going to throw you another fastball. It'll be a little faster than the last one." Again Josh swung and missed. The fans watched eagerly.

Finally Satchel called: "I'm going to throw you another fastball, but it will be even faster than the last one. I'm not going to throw any smoke around your yoke. It'll be a pea around your knee." He looked, then fired. Strike three. Satchel had struck out Josh and won the bet.

In 1942 Satchel's annual salary was $37,000, a huge sum at that time. After Hank Greenberg went into the military service, Satchel became the highest-paid player in baseball. Although it had been a long time since Satchel was a poor black child with barely enough food and little apparent ability to better himself, the feelings he had at that time were deeply etched inside of him. It was not enough for Satchel to know that he was the highest-paid baseball player. He wanted to show he had "made good" by buying antiques and fine china and other expensive items. Then, when people saw that he owned the oldest or the most expensive things or drove a fancy Cadillac, they would realize that he was wealthy and successful. The possessions helped him prove to himself that he really was an important person.

Although Satchel was anxious to earn as much money as possible by playing every chance he got, he took a stand against the discrimination he faced daily. He refused to play in a town if he could not eat there or stay in a hotel there. Promoters were warned about this beforehand and sometimes people at the local Chamber of Commerce would make room arrangements for him.

People were eager to see Satchel play and tried to

accommodate him. They were especially interested in seeing the pitch he'd developed in 1943. Satchel called it his hesitation pitch. He stood on the mound and stretched, keeping his arms over his head a little longer than usual. Then he put his left foot forward, but did not bring his arm around right away. He put his foot down and stopped for a second before he threw the ball. Batters began to swing while he was still holding the ball. Opponents complained that the pitch was illegal, but it was upheld by the umpire.

Satchel still did not get to all the games on time and sometimes he did not get there at all. But he claimed that he was accused of skipping more games than he actually did. Sometimes he was invited to make a guest appearance, but the promoter would not send the money that Satchel required in advance. Still, the promoter advertised that Satchel was pitching. Or when it was not Satchel's turn to pitch, promoters sometimes advertised anyway that Satchel was going to pitch. This was done in order to bring in the crowds. Then the sportswriters blamed Satchel for letting down the fans.

One day when Satchel had not been scheduled to pitch, an editorial said: "The great Satchel . . . the man who has received more than any other player in Negro baseball for doing less, didn't feel like putting on his uniform. He didn't feel like giving the fans who had trudged out to Forbes Field a 'break.' So he just lolled around the dressing room while his mates were out on the field taking a shellacking from the Homestead Grays." Satchel felt frustrated, but he said it did no good to argue.

He hoped this kind of publicity would not hurt his chances to get into the major leagues when they became open to blacks. He wondered when that would be. Rumors were strong that it would be soon. This was not the first time there had been such talk. But for Satchel, who was approaching forty, time was running out.

7

THE COLOR LINE

There was no written rule that blacks could not play in the major leagues. But there was an unwritten agreement and most of the club owners in the early 1940s did not hire black players. But one man developed a plan.

In 1943 Bill Veeck arranged to buy the Philadelphia Phillies from owner Jerry Nugent. Although Veeck did not tell Nugent, he intended to hire a team composed entirely of black players for the Phillies—a team including Satchel Paige. He told only his partner, Rudy Schaeffer, the editor of the *Pittsburgh Courier*, Wendell Smith, and promoter Abe Saperstein about the plan.

At the last minute Veeck decided he should tell Baseball Commissioner Kenesaw Mountain Landis that he was going to hire black ball players. When they got together in Chicago, Landis was polite and friendly. However, after Veeck left, he told Nugent not to sell the Phillies to Bill Veeck. By the time Veeck returned home, Nugent had sold the team to someone else for half as much money as Veeck had agreed to pay.

That same year Branch Rickey, the new general manager of the National League's Brooklyn Dodgers, told his scouts to start looking for good black players. He knew about Veeck's experience and was secretive about his plans.

When Satchel heard rumors about the efforts of Veeck and Rickey to get blacks into the major leagues, he hoped something would happen soon. He was thirty-seven, and most players his age had lost a lot of their baseball skills. He worried about how much longer his pitching arm would last.

But, in 1943, Satchel was still an outstanding pitcher, and in July, the Chicago fans decided to honor him. They scheduled a Satchel Paige Day at Wrigley Field on a day when he was pitching for the Memphis Red Sox against the New York Cubans. The newspapers advertised the game. But the game was not the only item about Satchel in the papers. There was also a notice that Janet Howard Paige, whom he had not seen since 1939, had filed for a divorce. After he pitched against the Cubans and was honored before 25,000 people, a man stopped him on the way out of the ballpark and gave him a divorce summons. On August 4, the divorce was granted by the court.

Satchel didn't have time to mope around. He had the 1943 East-West game at Comiskey Park in Chicago to think about. Nearly 52,000 fans attended the game, and another 10,000 were turned away.

After the United States entered World War II, Satchel had tried to enlist in the U.S. Army, but he was too old, so he contributed to the war effort by visiting army hospitals and camps. Some wounded sailors in a naval hospital in San Diego especially wanted to see Satchel. As they lay on stretchers, they touched his amazing arm. In a San Francisco hospital, he met a soldier he had played against on the House of David team and reminisced about the games they played in together.

Satchel thought about the wounded soldiers a lot. In 1944 he decided to see if the Negro League East-West

All-Star game could be played as a benefit for them. He asked many of the managers and the club owners, but they were not enthusiastic. When it came time to pick the all-stars that year, Satchel talked to reporters, who also thought it was a good idea. The owners told reporters they depended on the income from the all-star game to break even for the season. Satchel said unless they played the game for the soldiers, he would not play in it. The managers and owners still refused, and Satchel stayed home from the game. So did a lot of fans.

Although he wasn't in the East-West game in 1944, Satchel had an excellent year and earned a lot of money. He spent a lot too, buying cars and fishing and hunting equipment. Lahoma Brown, a lady from Kansas City whom he dated, hated to see Satchel squander his money and encouraged him to invest in property. Satchel listened to her and bought a big house in Kansas City.

In 1945, while Satchel was playing with the Kansas City Monarchs, rumors were stronger than ever that major league teams were on the verge of hiring black players and that Satchel was the most likely candidate. Satchel put all his effort into pitching for the Monarchs, who had another good team. One of the team's best rookies that year was a college-educated player named Jackie Robinson.

After the Monarchs' season finished, the Satchel Paige All-Stars barnstormed against the team led by Bob Feller, who had just returned from the service. Satchel missed one of the early games, and Feller, who was organizing the whole tour, hired Negro-Leaguer Chet Brewer for a hundred dollars a day plus expenses to make sure Satchel got to all the games.

In October they were playing around San Francisco, and every day they listened to the World Series game before going off to play their own game. On the day of the seventh game of the Series Satchel and Bob Feller sat in the St. Francis Hotel in San Francisco listening to the game. As the Tigers defeated the Cubs, Satchel day-dreamed about pitching in the World Series, striking out batter after batter. He had a passion to play in the Series.

While Satchel was still on the West Coast, Dodger owner Branch Rickey announced that he had signed Satchel's teammate, Jackie Robinson, and assigned him to a minor league team, the Montreal Royals of the International League. Jackie was to begin playing for the Royals in 1946. Rickey's scouts had considered Satchel, but they thought Robinson would be better as the first black in organized baseball because of his personality and education.

Satchel was angry and frustrated. He had been the one who opened major league parks to blacks. He had been the one the major league players wanted to barnstorm against. All these years everyone said that he belonged in the major leagues. But now it seemed that the door to organized baseball was opening too late for Satchel Paige.

That winter Satchel read the articles about Jackie Robinson. Everyone was anxious to see how he would do in the International League, which was just a notch below the major leagues. With all the attention on Jackie, Satchel wondered about himself. Had the major league owners forgotten about him? He hoped that somehow he could skip the minor leagues and beat Jackie to the majors. Satchel threw hard all season, hoping that a major league team would call him—but none did. He promised himself he would keep throwing until someone realized they needed him.

Satchel barnstormed against Bob Feller again after the 1946 major league season. The top Negro leaguers and the top major leaguers traveled coast to coast in two DC-7s and played very closely contested ball games. They played two games in Yankee Stadium in early October and drew 100,000 people, then traveled all over the North.

"We did not play against the blacks in the South in those days," Feller said. "It could not be done."

Satchel and Bob Feller usually pitched the first four or five innings. Then Bob Lemon often took over for Feller and Hilton Smith replaced Satchel. The last games of the tour were in California. At a game in old Wrigley Field in Los Angeles, thousands of people had to be turned away. Pitcher Bob Lemon's mother couldn't even get a seat. "We almost had a riot outside," Feller said. "We had to hold the game up about an hour and a half to sell the tickets. People who attend exhibition games don't buy tickets far in advance. They want to see how the weather is and how much money they have and what else they have to do. I had Max Patkin the clown and Jackie Price keep the fans entertained until we could get everyone into the park. Price caught fly balls in a jeep and performed other tricks."

Barnstorming brought in a lot of money for the players. The two all-star teams drew over 400,000 fans in the month they played against each other in 1946. Bob Feller paid each of his players $10,000 for the tour. Major leaguer Stan Musial missed several games during the first part of the tour because he had played in the World Series that year, but Feller paid him a full share for participating. Later that fall, Musial criticized the major league club owners for not paying more money to the players. He said he could earn more barnstorming against the black all-stars than he could by playing in the World Series. Feller said that statement "scared the heck out of the league."

Satchel wondered how long the barnstorming would last once blacks started to play in the major leagues. He prayed that a major league team would call him soon.

8

ROOKIE AGAIN

In 1947 Jackie Robinson was called up to play for the Brooklyn Dodgers and became the first black player in the major leagues. Satchel lost out again. He wondered if his good pitching arm would last long enough for him to make the majors at all.

That season Bill Veeck, president of the Cleveland Indians, asked Satchel's friend, Abe Saperstein, if Satchel was still a strong pitcher. Saperstein assured him that he was. Still, Veeck was hesitant to hire Satchel as the first black player in the American League. Both Veeck and Satchel were showmen, and Veeck was afraid that if he signed Satchel, people would think he was doing it as a publicity stunt. That would have been nothing new for Veeck, but he didn't want to do anything that might hurt the cause of blacks in the majors.

Satchel heard about Veeck's inquiries. After Veeck, who needed an outfielder, signed Negro Leaguer Larry Doby Satchel sent Veeck a telegram asking, "Is it time for me to come?"

56

Veeck wired back, "All things in due time."

Satchel hoped that time would come soon. Lahoma Brown constantly encouraged him in his baseball career. He decided not to let her get away, and married her October 12, 1947 in Hayes, Kansas. Lahoma had a daughter, Shirley Long, from her previous marriage. In the next five years, they added four more children to their family: Pamela in 1948, Carolyn in 1949, Linda in 1951, and Robert in 1952. In 1958 they had Lula and finally in 1960, their last child, Rita. Satchel's family meant a lot to him. And, although he was always willing to give the press a story about his pitching, he protected his family from the media. Reporters knew they were not free to question him about his private life.

In 1948 Satchel's earnings fell drastically. With more blacks in the majors, attendance slacked off at Negro League games. Satchel impatiently waited for a call from a major league club.

Meanwhile the Cleveland Indians were in the 1948 pennant race and were desperate for pitching help. Bill Veeck asked Cleveland pitcher, Bob Feller, if he thought Satchel still had major league pitching ability.

"He had it the last time I saw him," Feller told Veeck. "I think he could help us a lot." Satchel had performed superbly in the postseason tour in 1947, striking out fifteen major leaguers in one game.

Cleveland manager Lou Boudreau was skeptical. He heard that Satchel had lost a lot of his speed. In spite of Boudreau's reservations, Veeck contacted Abe Saperstein and asked him to bring Satchel to Cleveland for a tryout. Satchel and Lahoma danced all over the house when Saperstein's letter came.

Satchel arrived in Cleveland on his "official" forty-second birthday, July 7, 1948. Veeck had seen Satchel during his barnstorming days. As a kid, he had watched Satchel face Dizzy Dean in the famous 13-inning game that Satchel won 1–0. He knew Satchel was at his best

*After years of rejection, Satchel crossed
the color line in the major leagues in 1948,
and was contracted by Bill Veeck to pitch
for the Cleveland Indians.*

when something was at stake. Before asking him to pitch to manager Boudreau, Veeck took Satchel aside. "It's important to me that you look good against this guy," he said. "I've been telling everybody you're the best player in baseball. Now's the chance to prove it."

"Don't worry, Mr. Will." Satchel said. "I been there before."

Lou Boudreau came out in his uniform. "Can you still pitch like you used to?" he asked Satchel.

"I got as fast a ball as anybody pitching now, but I have to admit it's not half as fast as it used to be. But I got control."

Boudreau put on a catcher's mitt and stood behind the plate. "All right, see if you can get it up here." Satchel tossed a couple of easy throws, then he fired in pitch after pitch.

After a while Boudreau stepped out from behind the plate. "That's some control. You didn't miss the strike zone more than four times out of fifty." He took off his glove: "Let's see how you do when I bat against you."

Boudreau was leading both leagues with a batting average of nearly .400. Satchel threw him twenty pitches. Nineteen of them were strikes and the other was a pop fly.

He had easily passed his tryout, and Veeck took him to the clubhouse and signed him up. Satchel was now a major leaguer. His dream had come true. He was reportedly paid ten thousand dollars to play the second half of the season. The fans were excited about Satchel making the big leagues. Reporters called him at all hours. "Do you think you can last in the majors?" they asked.

"The plate's the same size," Satchel answered.

But, as Veeck had feared, some people saw the signing of Paige as a publicity stunt. Considering how close the pennant race was, Veeck was surprised at such a reaction. He could hardly believe that people would think a first-place team like the Cleveland Indians would hire someone for any reason other than to help the team win the pennant.

The *Sporting News* carried editorials against bringing someone as old as Satchel into the major leagues. J. G. Taylor wrote:

Many . . . fail to see eye to eye with the signing of Satchel Paige. . . . To bring in a pitching rookie of Paige's age . . . is to demean the standards of baseball in the big circuits.

"I demeaned the big circuits considerable that year," Paige said later. "I won six and lost one."

Two days after joining the Indians, Satchel became the first black to pitch in the American League when he played a relief role against the St. Louis Browns at Cleveland's Municipal Stadium.

Starting pitcher Bob Lemon was behind four to one in the fifth inning. Before the sixth inning began, the words "SATCHEL . . . LEROY . . . PAIGE" came over the public-address system. Fans were on their feet. They kept cheering as Satchel took his long, slow walk to the mound. Just the sight of the tall, thin figure sauntering onto the field was exciting. This was the famous Satchel Paige, who had probably won more games than anyone else in baseball history.

Colliers magazine stated: "The night that Paige walked out of a quarter century of circus baseball into the rarified atmosphere of the big leagues, some 20,000 fans at Cleveland stadium rose for ten minutes of unbroken roaring. Paige obliged by blanking the Browns for 2 innings."

Later Satchel said, "I wasn't afraid of anybody I had seen in that batter's box. I'd been around too long for that. I wasn't as fast as I used to be, but I was a better pitcher. If I couldn't overpower them, I'd outcute them."

Satchel spurred the Indians on. On July 14 he pitched

four scoreless innings against the Brooklyn Dodgers. At first he was used only as a relief pitcher. Then on August 20, he was called to start against Chicago. There were 78,382 fans in the stadium, more people than there had ever been at a major league night game.

Most of the players were already in the dressing room when Satchel got to the ballpark. He wasn't his usual relaxed self. His stomach was tense. If he could pitch a shutout, the Indians would tie the major league record of four shutouts in a row.

"This game is important to me," Veeck told him. "Really give it to them tonight."

Satchel had every intention of giving his best in that game. Later he said that his biggest thrill was that first game as the starting pitcher for a big league team with Feller and Lemon in the bullpen. "I was so proud, I grew two inches. I sure didn't want them to come and take me out of there. Man, did I bear down."

Feller and Lemon were never called on. Satchel pitched a shutout, giving up three hits, striking out five, and walking only one. He showed the crowd his hesitation pitch and other pitches for which he invented such names as the two-hump blooper and the bat dodger. The fans roared and stomped their feet as the game ended, and the players slapped him on the back and pumped his hand when he returned to the dugout.

Some major league batters thought he might be easy to bunt against. Satchel reported, "They were going to bunt me—old man me—out of the majors at first. But they soon quit when I tossed them out underhanded without looking to first base—a snap throw right after picking it up. Funny thing about that. I was accused of insulting the league. They said it was clowning that didn't belong in the majors. But an out's an out."

Satchel pitched well against many outstanding batters. "He was always very successful against Joe Di-

Maggio," teammate Bob Feller said. "Much more so than I ever was."

Bill Veeck said that whenever Paige and DiMaggio faced each other, "Satchel thought positively and DiMaggio thought negatively. Joe came to the plate. Satchel fooled around until Joe was nervous and anxious. He did his windmill windup, took his time, and talked to his catcher. By the time he threw the ball, Joe had lost his concentration."

As Satchel continued playing the usual questions about his age came up. When reporters asked him how old he was, Satchel gave each one a different answer.

Negro Leaguer Buck Leonard remembered hearing Satchel explain why there was such a mix-up about his age. "Once his mother went to the courthouse to tell them how old he was, and the man wrote it down wrong. At the time he didn't have an eraser on his pencil, so he couldn't change it. He said he would change it later, but he never did. So that was why there was confusion about his birthdate." Bill Veeck even hired a private detective to investigate Satchel's age, but the detective didn't come up with a definite age that Veeck had confidence in.

People wondered how Satchel would adjust to the strict time schedule of organized baseball after ignoring clocks and calendars while traveling on his own during his barnstorming years. With the Indians he missed a lot of trains, but he usually made it to the game. He memorized the plane schedules and if he didn't make the train, he hopped a flight.

Still, Satchel did not always arrive on time. Sometimes he was late because of transportation problems. Sometimes he blamed the weather. He said he could always tell what weather was coming by the way his big toe felt. One rainy day in New York he came into the clubhouse late. The canvas was on the field, but the game had not been called yet. Manager Boudreau was upset because Satchel arrived after the deadline.

"Well, I knew we weren't going to play," Satchel said. "When I woke up this morning, I could tell by the way my big toe was throbbing that the game would be called because of rain." It was.

The players accepted Satchel and made allowances for his idiosyncracies. "You couldn't have the same rules for Satchel as for the other players," Bob Feller said. "He would never run with the pitchers." When Boudreau talked to Satchel about it, he said, "I pitch with my arms, not my feet."

He was included in the team's practical jokes. "Satchel was not a real practical joker," Feller said, "but he was not against getting involved in a practical joke. For example, in the goodie box in Detroit, the ice cream bars had wafers around them, and the ice cream was just as white and just the same size as a bar of soap. Once I gave him a bar of soap with a Nabisco cracker on each side. Satchel bit into it and his artificial tooth went flying across the room. Satchel thought it was a great joke."

But Satchel was serious about his baseball, and he helped keep his team near the top in the league standings. At the end of August, the Indians were in the heat of the race for the pennant. On August 30 they had dropped two games out of first place and stood in third place. Satchel pitched against the Washington Senators and beat them, moving the Indians to one-and-a-half games back.

The pennant race was close right to the end. When the regularly scheduled games for the season were over, the Indians were tied for first place with the Boston Red Sox. The Indians won the play-off game, putting them in the 1948 World Series. Satchel might have a chance to play in the Series and fulfill another of his dreams. He had helped the Indians win the pennant and had a good record that season. In the twenty-one games in which he pitched, he won six, including a shutout, and lost only one.

As Bob Feller started against the Braves in game one

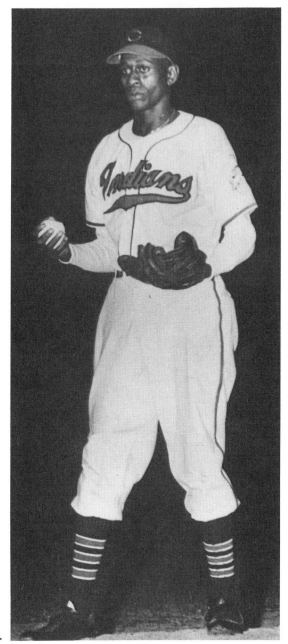

Satchel on the mound for the Indians in the 1948 World Series. He was named Rookie of the Year, the oldest rookie so honored in baseball history.

of the Series, Satchel was ready to come in if he was needed. But Feller's pitching was strong and he pitched the whole game, although the Indians lost 1–0.

In the second game Bob Lemon started for the Indians, and Satchel relaxed in the bullpen. As Lemon began to struggle, the fans yelled, "We want Satchel!" Satchel tried to hide his excitement when Boudreau signaled for him to warm up. But then Lemon settled down and stayed in to win the game.

The team headed back to Cleveland, and Veeck announced that Gene Bearden would be starting pitcher for game three. Bearden won game three in a shutout, and Satchel hoped he would pitch next. However, manager Boudreau put in Steve Gromek, who gave the Indians their third win of the four games. One more victory and the Series would be over. Fans and sportswriters were calling for Satchel to pitch.

"How about putting me in?" Satchel asked Boudreau. But Boudreau didn't commit himself. Finally he announced that Bob Feller would start the fifth game. Feller had been pitching so well that Satchel saw little hope of getting into the World Series. In the first inning the Braves got three runs from Feller, but Boudreau kept him in. The Indians scored some runs, and by the end of the fourth, they were leading five to four. In the seventh, after the Braves tied the game, Feller gave up a single.

Boudreau looked to the bull pen and signaled for Satchel, Klieman, and Christopher to start warming up. When the Braves went ahead, the crowd chanted for Satchel, but Boudreau waved in Klieman to replace Feller. Satchel was so disappointed that he felt like sitting down, but he kept throwing as Klieman walked two and gave up a single. Boudreau changed pitchers again. This time he brought in Christopher, who gave up two singles. With the Indians trailing 11–5, Boudreau signaled for Satchel and eighty-six thousand fans cheered him on as he sauntered to the mound.

There was a man on first and only one out. Satchel got the first man out, and began his windup to the second batter. He put his arms up then brought them down and rested them on his chest. The umpire called a balk. Satchel was angry about the call and got the batter out quickly to retire the side.

When the Indians came to bat, Satchel was taken out for a pinch hitter, giving him only two-thirds of an inning in the game. Although the Indians went on to win the World Series, they lost that game. Satchel's brief appearance made him the first black to pitch in a World Series. But for the rest of his life Satchel felt resentment at being given only a token appearance in the World Series.

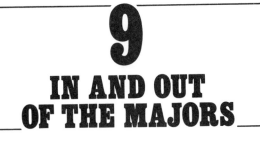

9
IN AND OUT
OF THE MAJORS

After the last World Series game in Boston, Satchel flew back to Cleveland with a couple of other Cleveland players instead of taking the train with the rest of the team. Bill Veeck reported that Satchel, who had a huge appetite, had finished two meals on the plane. As a joke, the flight attendant asked him if he would like another. Satchel said "Yes," and had no trouble eating that one, too.

As the flight attendant cleared away the dishes, she offered him a fourth meal.

"No, thanks," Satchel answered, pushing back the tray.

"Oh, you're full?" she asked.

"No," he said. "Just tired from all that eating."

The team split up after the season, and Satchel went on an exhibition tour. As he traveled, he was asked how he stayed so young, and he developed the following set of rules, which got written up by sports columnists on the East Coast:

- Avoid fried meats which angry up the blood.
- If your stomach disputes you, lie down and pacify it with cool thoughts.
- Keep the juices flowing by jangling around gently as you move.
- Go very lightly on the vices, such as carrying on in society—the social ramble ain't restful.
- Avoid running at all times.
- And don't look back. Something might be gaining on you.

But on October 24, 1948, Satchel did look back over his career as Los Angeles held a Satchel Paige Day. Satchel received a special Helms Award, then pitched three innings against his Cleveland Indians teammate, Gene Bearden.

When asked if he would play for Cleveland in 1949, he said it was up to the boss. The boss said "Yes," and Satchel received his contract for the season with the Indians on February 14, 1949. He went to spring training late that year. The *Arizona Daily Star* gave the reason: "Paige, oldster of the world champions, will go to Hot Springs, Arkansas shortly for a treatment of hot baths."

Then, a month later, the *Arizona Daily Star* reported: "Paige will give his ancient arm its first test of the season tomorrow when the Cleveland Indians play the Chicago Cubs in an exhibition game at Los Angeles.

"Satchel encountered a little difficulty yesterday when he missed the bus for San Bernardino. Apparently he won't draw a fine because Tribe manager Lou Boudreau said:

" 'As a matter of policy, I don't levy fines for such stunts during the training season. The fellows' salaries haven't started yet. But Satch will have to learn that the rules apply to him as well as to everyone else. I'm pretty sure he'll understand when I get through talking to him.' "

Satchel relaxed through most of spring training. Through all the years of pitching nearly every day, he had learned to conserve his strength.

As Satchel traveled with the Indians, reporters were always eager to interview him. "He made good copy," Bob Feller explained. "He gave everyone a different story."

One reporter had heard that Satchel once studied at Knoxville College and asked him if that were true.

"Well, you could say this," Satchel said. "You could say that I learned something in Knoxville one time."

"When?" the reporter asked.

"Not lately," Satchel replied, and went off to the dugout.

As the regular season started, Satchel's stomach began to bother him so much that it threw his pitching off. He kept a bottle of medicine with him to take whenever the "misery" hit. During the first four months of the season, the stomach pains would come and go, and his pitching varied—depending on how his stomach felt.

By August 7 he had four wins and five losses. As the month progressed his stomach bothered him so much that he was not able to pitch more than two or three innings a game. He couldn't win, and was charged with two more losses. Satchel worried about his record and wondered if his contract would be renewed.

When his physician examined him, he found nothing wrong with Satchel except his bad teeth, and sent him to a dentist. The dentist told him that all his teeth would have to come out.

"How will I eat?" Satchel asked.

"I'll put in false teeth."

"Doctor, I will not abide with store teeth," Paige said.

"Then you will not abide," the dentist answered.

Satchel finally had the teeth pulled and began to feel better. He was ready for the 1950 season, but Veeck had left the Indians, and things were not as smooth with the new administration. Hank Greenberg, the new general manager, told Satchel they couldn't use him.

Satchel had not expected to be dropped and went home and moped around the house for days. Then he called Ralph Wilkinson, the former owner of the Kansas City Monarchs, and asked if he could help him get independent bookings. Satchel did not want to sign with a team. "I want to stay loose so those big boys can call me if they want to," he explained.

Both Wilkinson and Abe Saperstein worked on getting bookings for him. Once the word was out that Satchel was available, offers came pouring in. Satchel went back to sleeping in his car and playing in parks in small towns. It was a comedown for him after playing in the major leagues, but he earned good money.

Bill Veeck told Satchel not to worry. He said that he would be back in the majors soon, and when that happened there would be a place for Satchel. In July 1951 Veeck bought the St. Louis Browns and asked Satchel to join the team on July 17. Veeck bought Satchel a contour chair with an awning that had Satchel's name on it and put it in the bull pen, as a place for Satchel to relax. Although he had just passed his "official" forty-fourth birthday, Satchel told reporters he was forty-two.

"Satchel just drops his age a couple of years each season," Veeck explained.

But mostly, reporters were interested in Satchel's pitching. A writer for *The New Yorker* described one of

After being dropped from the major leagues during the 1950 season, Satchel returned in 1951 to play for the St. Louis Browns and, again, for new owner and old friend Bill Veeck, who presented Satchel with his new uniform.

his pitches this way: "He winds up with agonizing deliberation. Then, as he nears the end of his throwing motion, he stops the forward movement of his arm so the ball just trickles toward home plate. It's the only pitch with sound accompaniment. He slaps his left foot down hard, just before unclasping the ball."

Bill Durney, road secretary for the Browns, told reporters Satchel could throw a ball about twelve ways and had four ways of winding up. He also said Satchel was the slowest pitcher in baseball.

"Too many pitchers got the hurry-ups," Satchel explained. "When I talk to young pitchers, I tell them to slow down. You last longer."

Satchel was a great strategist and used psychology to help get batters out. Sometimes he would throw three straight balls to the batter, then act like he couldn't get anything over the plate. Then when the batter became careless, Satchel would strike him out. Although Satchel couldn't throw hard for as many innings as he did when he was younger, he had the speed when he needed it. Veeck said, "In a tight spot, on any given pitch, he can throw much harder than any pitcher today." Satchel found the pitch that worked for the batters he faced, then saved it for those tight spots.

Satchel still had his control. Catcher Chuck Courtney was amazed by Satchel's ability to throw the ball exactly where he wanted it. "You hear about pinpoint control," he said. "But Satchel is the only man I've ever seen who

In 1951 against the Detroit Tigers, Satchel pitched one of his most thrilling games, an extra-innings shutout. During that same season, Satchel was appointed to the American League All-Star team.

72

has it. Once he threw me six strikes out of ten pitches over a gum wrapper."

In 1951 the fans were just as intrigued by Satchel as the 1924 fans had been. Even when he got up from his seat in the bull pen to get a drink of water, the crowd buzzed with excitement.

In the two months he played for the St. Louis Browns in 1951, Satchel pitched in 23 games. He struck out 48 players in 62 innings and had a record of three wins and four losses with the last place team.

In 1952, he was back with the Browns. "If my legs hold out," he said, "I can stay up here (in the majors) another ten years. Man, I'm a hundred years old and I can still strike these guys out."

By August, Satchel had seven wins and six losses. On August 6, he was the starting pitcher against the Detroit Tigers. He threw hard and well, but the Detroit pitcher was also doing a good job. At the end of the ninth, the score was tied nothing to nothing. Detroit put in a relief pitcher.

In the tenth, Satchel loaded the bases with no outs and then got the next two batters to ground out in force plays. Then he struck out the third batter. Finally, in the twelfth, the Browns scored and won the game 1–0.

Sometimes teams would try to build up their score before Satchel came in to relieve the starting pitcher. If Casey Stengel, manager of the New York Yankees, didn't think his players were taking their game against the Browns seriously, he would warn them about Satchel. "Get the runs now," he said, "Father Time is coming."

Satchel won 12 games and lost 10 for the last-place St. Louis Browns in 1952. He saved 10 other games and struck out 91 batters.

But in 1953 Satchel could not seem to win. He had a 3–9 record, the worst he had ever had. Before the 1954 season Veeck sold the St. Louis Browns and the team moved to Baltimore. The new owners said they were starting a youth movement and didn't have room for Satchel, who would "officially" be forty-eight that year. Satchel wondered if he would ever play major league baseball again.

10
ON THE
ROAD AGAIN

Satchel went back to barnstorming in 1954 and pitched in 154 games. The next year he played for the Kansas City Monarchs, but he didn't make the big money he had made eight years earlier. The Negro leagues were dying. The fans could now see blacks play in major league games and watch baseball on television.

During the 1955 season, the Monarchs could not play in Old Blues Stadium, the ballpark they had been renting. A major league team, the Athletics, moved to Kansas City from Philadelphia and took over the ballpark, renaming it Municipal Stadium. Without a home ballpark the Monarchs became exclusively a traveling team. It was rumored that they would quit the following year, and Satchel, who was nearly fifty, wondered what he would do for a living.

Then, in 1956, he received another call from Bill Veeck. Veeck had become vice president of the Miami Marlins, a team in the International League, and he wanted Satchel to pitch for him. Although the Monarchs did not quit despite all the rumors, Satchel jumped at the chance to return to organized baseball.

It was Miami's first year in the International League, and Veeck started off the season with a bang. On opening night, Satchel flew into the ballpark in a helicopter. He came out of the plane, threw a few balls, then went to the bull pen and plopped into the rocking chair—which Veeck had waiting for him. He spent the rest of the night there. When Satchel finally pitched his first game for the Miami Marlins, he shut out Montreal, the defending champions.

Lahoma and the children liked living in Miami. They could go swimming every day, and the people made them feel like celebrities. And for Satchel, there was plenty of fishing between games.

In August 1956, Veeck planned a special promotion for the Marlins, which he called: "The baseball party to end all baseball parties." He rented the Orange Bowl, a football stadium in Miami, and billed Satchel as the starting pitcher against the Columbus Jets. He hired famous entertainers of the day to perform—people like Cab Calloway and Margaret Whiting.

As Satchel went onto the field to warm up, 51,713 fans filled the stadium. "See all them folks out there," Satchel said to his manager. "They're really gonna see a show now." And they did. In the first six innings Satchel gave up only two hits and no runs. But by the eighth inning he was exhausted. The relief pitcher got the last four men out and Satchel was credited with the victory. Altogether, Satchel had eleven wins for the Marlins in 1956 with only four losses, and he had an ERA (earned run average) of 1.86.

Although Bill Veeck left the Marlins the following year, Satchel stayed on through 1958. He played well, but he did not get along with the new managers and said he would not return for the 1959 season. Lahoma understood Satchel's feelings; still, she worried about where the money would come from to support their family.

Satchel felt frustrated. He didn't want to put up with problems with the managers, but the idea of giving up organized baseball to go back on the road and scratch for a living was not appealing either. Then he was offered a role in a cowboy movie called *The Wonderful Country*. On September 30 Satchel signed for the part of a cavalry sergeant. He could hardly wait to finish with the Miami Marlins and leave for Durango, Mexico for the filming.

As soon as the season ended, Satchel packed up his family and went to Mexico to begin his movie career. He liked the acting, but he had to ride a horse, and he kept falling off. With the help of some Hollywood stuntmen, Satchel developed enough skill to stay on the horse. Satchel felt encouraged when the film director told him that he was such a good actor he would be offered plenty of movie roles. Satchel had always loved to perform and had dreamed of becoming a star. But months went by without any offers.

Finally he gave up and accepted some barnstorming invitations. Satchel continued to pitch on the road for the next two seasons. Toward the end of 1961, the Portland Beavers, members of the Pacific Coast League, hired him to finish their season. At age fifty-five Satchel was still a strong enough pitcher to play in the league. In the 25 innings he pitched for them, he had 19 strikeouts and had an ERA of 2.88. "Maybe I'll pitch forever," he said.

In 1962, Satchel pitched more than 200 innings for the Kansas City Monarchs, playing one-nighters from coast to coast. That year, Jackie Robinson was the first black

After three years of playing in the minor leagues again, the always appealing Satchel appeared as a U.S. Cavalry sergeant in the 1958 movie, The Wonderful Country.

baseball player inducted into the Baseball Hall of Fame. The news about Jackie was hard for Satchel to bear. Baseball writers had talked about putting him in the Hall of Fame long before the public had ever heard of Jackie Robinson.

Satchel wondered if he would ever be voted in. He could not meet the requirement of ten years in the major leagues because he had not been allowed to play in organized baseball early enough in his career. Sportswriters argued that the Baseball Hall of Fame executives should give black players credit for their years in the Negro leagues, but Hall of Fame executives said no.

In the mid-sixties Satchel was still working hard for a living, finding pitching jobs wherever he could in order to support his family. Many of the former superstars in the major leagues, whom Satchel had beaten in his prime, had retired and were receiving baseball pensions, but Satchel could not qualify for even the minimum pension. He had not played in the big leagues for the required length of time. He continued to ride on the rickety bus or drive his station wagon from place to place, pitching an inning or two for the barnstorming clubs. He slept in his car or stayed in a run-down hotel.

"I do all my own cooking right beside the road," Satchel said in a 1965 interview. "I keep the station wagon stocked up with everything I need. I just bought me a brand new Coleman stove."

But between hops he loved to come home to Lahoma's cooking. Satchel said Lahoma was one of the best cooks in the world. He loved being with his family and relaxing around his house on Twenty-fourth Street in Kansas City. It was a two-story brick-and-frame house, with high ceilings, dark woodwork, and a heavy staircase. The dining room was filled with his trophies, awards, and framed testimonials to his accomplishments. He enjoyed the shade of the big elm tree in the backyard which helped keep the house cool in the blazing summers. He was glad he owned the house. His barnstorming money and Lahoma's salary from working in a pastry shop was all they had to live on.

In September of 1965 it seemed that Satchel's luck was about to change. Charlie Finley, owner of the Kansas City Athletics, signed him on as a pitcher. This was Satchel's first major league contract in twelve years. Finley did not make it clear whether he would keep Satchel on the roster after the season ended. He only stated, "We'll be interested in signing him for 1966."

The city council of Kansas City proclaimed September 25, 1965 as Satchel Paige Day. Satchel was overwhelmed with emotion as he came out of the city hall council chamber with the proclamation in his hand. Former Negro leaguer Buck O'Neil was on hand. "He's the last one," O'Neil said. "He's a link to a time when baseball was something else than what it is today . . ."

That night Satchel was the starting pitcher against the Boston Red Sox. He used only 28 pitches to shut out the Red Sox for the first three innings. He did not walk a single batter, and he gave up only one hit. Writing about 59-year-old Satchel, *Kansas City Star* reporter Paul O'Boynick said, "It was almost unbelievable to watch Paige mow down the Boston hitters. He used fastballs, curves, and his famous hesitation pitch . . . the amazing part was his fastball. The Red Sox players were surprised that he could throw that fast."

Finley took Satchel out after the third inning. No one was really sure why. As he returned to the dugout, Satchel doffed his cap to over 9,000 cheering fans. After he had gone to the clubhouse, someone rushed in and yelled, "They want you back on the field." In honor of Satchel Paige Day, the stadium lights were turned out and 9,000 matches were lighted. The crowd sang good-bye to him with "Rocking Chair," "Silver Threads Among the Gold," and "The Old Gray Mare, She Ain't What She Used To Be."

Back in the clubhouse, Satchel said "The Old Gray

Mare just might be what she used to be." He was just getting warmed up, and he hoped to help the Athletics a lot. But seventeen days after he was signed, Satchel was let go. People said Finley had brought him in at the end of the 1965 season to create interest in his last-place ball club. Another chance for Satchel to earn his pension had slipped away.

He went back to pitching, mainly in command performances. Even when he "officially" turned sixty, his presence could still fill a ballpark. Baseball promoters were eager to book him, and Satchel kept on pitching all over the United States and Canada. As he said, "Old green was hard to hold onto."

Talk of getting Satchel into the Baseball Hall of Fame continued. When Ted Williams was inducted into the Cooperstown museum in 1966, he said: "I hope that someday Satchel Paige and Josh Gibson will be voted into the Hall of Fame as symbols of the great Negro players who are not here only because they were not given a chance to play."

In 1967 Satchel toured with the Indianapolis Clowns, a former Negro League team which now had both black and white players. He was paid $1,000 a month and given a $500 bonus for appearances in major league parks.

While playing for the Clowns, Satchel usually pitched only the last three innings and had plenty of time for fishing. He often fished along the river nearest to the ballpark during the first few innings. Then, midway through the game, owner Ed Hamman would go to the river himself or send one of the players to get Satchel, who was already in uniform. Sometimes he gave the fish to the umpire as a joke.

Satchel headed west after his season with the Clowns. While he was pitching for an all-star team around Seattle, a scout for the Atlanta Braves watched him play. Satchel had a feeling he would hear from the Braves, but months went by and he heard nothing.

Although other blacks were getting on the baseball pension plan, Satchel still lacked the 158 days necessary to receive the minimum pension. It looked as though Roy Campanella would be the second black inducted into the Hall of Fame. Satchel felt like a forgotten man.

11

ATLANTA TO
COOPERSTOWN

Late in the summer of 1968 Satchel finally got the call
he'd been expecting from the Atlanta Braves. The scout
who saw him play in Washington had recommended him,
and Satchel was invited to join the team as a pitching
coach and possible pitcher. The job would give him the
158 days he needed to receive the baseball players pension. People suspected, however, that the Braves were
not just trying to help him earn his pension. Satchel could
still bring in the fans. He was excited about being back in
the major leagues. "This is my love," he said. "I'm glad
to be back with my love."

The *New York Times* quoted the Braves owner as
saying, "Satchel is one of the greatest pitchers of all time.
Baseball would be guilty of negligence should it not assure
this legendary figure a place in the pension plan. With his
tremendous background, Paige is expected to be a great
help in working with young pitchers. He may even get
into a game or two. We expect him to get into shape and
be ready to pitch." The management said there would be
no special chairs in the bull pen like the one in Miami.

During the sixties, Satchel was called on as a pitching coach in addition to being a sometime reliever. His advice to rookie players was invaluable. Here, Satchel demonstrates his techniques to four young Kansas City rookies including the now famous Hall of Famer Jim "Catfish" Hunter (right of Satchel).

As usual, Satchel's age was a big issue with reporters, and they kept checking for his true birth date. Satchel wasn't satisfied with the reports that his age had been established as sixty-two. "They've done a lot of investigating," he said. "And to tell the truth, it's got to where it puzzles me myself. They couldn't find my record in Mobile, because the jail had moved, and the judge had died."

Satchel reported to the Braves in Richmond, where they were playing against Atlanta's top farm team. The Braves' manager told the press, "Right now he's a pitcher. He's one of our twenty-five active players. Now I've got to find out if he can still pitch."

This time Satchel wasn't so sure of his pitching ability. "It depends on how things jiggle," he said. "I haven't touched a ball this season. I just have to get out there and see how I unfold. I got bloopers, loopers, and droopers. I got a jump ball, a screwball, a wobbly ball, a hurry-up ball, a nothin' ball, and a bat dodger. If I can throw half as good as I did last year, then I know I can still get them out."

Satchel's uniform displayed the number 65. This signified that when Paige reached age sixty-five, he would qualify for a pension. When asked how anyone would know when Satchel reached sixty-five, a Braves executive said that the league's office would just pick an official age.

Satchel was a great help on the coaching staff. During spring training the next year, Satchel got into an exhibition game and pitched a scoreless inning as Atlanta defeated Savannah 1–0. He gave up a lead-off double, then he got the next three batters out on a pop fly and two strikeouts. At sixty-three, he was proud to pitch that well for a major league team.

Satchel had finally earned the 158 days he needed to get on the baseball pension plan. Although the five years made him eligible only for the minimum pension of $250 a month, he needed the money, and felt honored to be included in the pension plan. He had overcome another hurdle and now turned his attention to discussions about the Baseball Hall of Fame.

Sportswriters continued to push for the inclusion of players from the Negro leagues in the Hall of Fame. Before the 1969 Hall of Fame ceremony, when black major leaguer Roy Campanella was to be inducted, Dick Young, president of the baseball writer's association, asked Campanella how many men from the Negro leagues should be included in the Hall of Fame. Campanella said about nine or ten, and Monte Irvin, another man who had played in both the Negro leagues and the major leagues, agreed.

At the Hall of Fame ceremony Young said that the writers' association would work to have the top Negro leaguers voted into the Hall of Fame and—try to "right the wrongs" that had been done.

Satchel followed the baseball writers' campaign eagerly over the next two years as they worked to have Hall of Fame officials change the rules and include outstanding Negro league players. The writers even threatened to withdraw their voting support from the Cooperstown Museum and start their own Hall of Fame. That brought action. A committee made up of people who had been part of the Negro leagues was set up to select black baseball stars.

On February 3, 1971, the *New York Times* reported: "A ten man committee composed of 8 Negroes and 2 white men, will name one player a year from the days before 1947, when Jackie Robinson joined the Brooklyn Dodgers and became the first black man in the big leagues.

"The first one will be picked next week and will enter the Hall of Fame at Cooperstown, New York, next August, as part of a new exhibit commemorating the contributions of the Negro leagues to baseball.

"The tablets honoring the black stars will be separate from the 117 that have been placed in the museum during the last 33 years. They included those for Jackie Robinson

(1962) and Roy Campanella (1969), the two (black players) who have been elected since baseball was integrated.

"To be elected to the Hall of Fame requires 10 years in the majors. For the new exhibit they will need to have been in the Negro leagues for at least ten years."

Satchel prayed that he would be the player chosen the following week. He knew that many people thought he should be first Negro leaguer in the Hall of Fame, but he had been disappointed so many times before that he wasn't sure what would happen. He waited anxiously for the decision.

This time he was not disappointed. The committee made him their first choice. Satchel and Lahoma went to Cooperstown where the announcement was to be made publicly on February 11, 1971. As Satchel stood with Lahoma before the press, reporters' questions pointed out the injustices of the past segregation in baseball and even the current segregation in the Hall of Fame.

"How did you feel about being excluded from the major leagues all those years?" they asked Satchel.

"I felt I had a world of my own out there," he said. "We were playing all over the world just like the white players. We were drawing thirty to sixty thousand people. And I was satisfied in my world the way it was."

They asked if he thought Jackie Robinson should have been the first black in the majors. "They said they had to have a college boy as the first black player in the big leagues," Satchel said. "And in my soul I believed Jackie should have been first."

Baseball Commissioner Bowie Kuhn
congratulates Satchel Paige upon
his induction into Baseball's
Hall of Fame in August 1971.

The writers continued pounding out their questions. They asked if he was bothered that the Negro leaguers would be segregated from the major leaguers in the Hall of Fame. How did he feel about being put in a separate wing of the Hall of Fame from the major leaguers he had beaten? Did he think baseball could do better now? Did he think any real progress had been made?

Satchel hesitated. What had started as a happy day for him was becoming cloudy. For a moment he felt confused.

"I don't feel segregated," he said.

There was tension in the air as the racial questions continued. Satchel's jaw tightened. Then Baseball Commissioner Bowie Kuhn stepped in to lighten the atmosphere. He changed the topic to Satchel's age and his next birthday. Was it August? July? What year? Satchel relaxed and smiled again.

But many people were not satisfied with the idea of putting the Negro leagues exhibit in a separate part of the museum from the tablets of the major league stars. One writer called it an "instant ghetto." Even a committee member said: "Sure it's tokenism." And some blacks challenged Satchel to reject the honor as "too little and too late, an easy way to ease the white man's conscience." Satchel seemed to be caught in the middle of the dispute.

Ebony Magazine criticized the move, saying: "To be seen in a separate exhibit—separate as always . . . is a hollow victory. The fact that he wasn't in the major leagues ten years was not his choice. It was not lack of talent."

The criticism caused the baseball commissioner's office and the Hall of Fame executives to change their plan. On July 7, 1971 the *Los Angeles Times* announced: "In response to severe criticism of this separate but equal treatment, Baseball Commissioner Bowie Kuhn and Paul Kerr, president of the National Baseball Hall of Fame and Museum at Cooperstown, New York, said Satchel and future Negro League inductees would be given full membership." Their bronze likenesses were to be placed in the Hall of Fame proper along with Babe Ruth, Ty Cobb, and all the others.

In August, 1971 Satchel was officially inducted into the Hall of Fame. He was glad the argument had been settled, and he was filled with happiness at being honored with the stars he had played with throughout the years. He looked out over the crowd at Cooperstown and said: "I am the proudest man on the face of the earth today."

12

THE FINAL INNING

The special Hall of Fame committee selected eight other Negro leaguers over the years, then disbanded. Satchel continued to make personal appearances at various places. After his induction into the Hall of Fame he was in greater demand than ever before. Sometimes he threw out the first ball at a game or signed autographs at a semipro tournament. Other times he told a few stories at a dinner or dedicated a ballpark. He often pitched an inning or two. "In hot weather I can still crank up," he said.

He wanted to work as a pitching coach, but no team hired him. *Life* magazine quoted Satchel as saying: "If there isn't one team that thinks I could make a good coach, well, I have to laugh." The editor went on to speculate that Satchel was not hired as a coach because of "his reputation of being unpredictable, not a virtue in a business where changing the color of the uniform is considered revolutionary."

In the 1970s, Satchel worked as a sales and promotion director for his friend, A. Ray Smith, owner of the Tulsa

Oilers. His body began to fail, but he kept promoting baseball. He developed emphysema, and by 1980 he was using oxygen to ease the discomfort. Later he had heart problems.

In 1981 Satchel was invited to Kentucky for a reunion of players from the Negro baseball leagues. A group at Ashland, Kentucky hoped to build a Negro Baseball Hall of History there. The reunion conflicted with an invitation to meet with President Reagan. Satchel talked with Lahoma before deciding which to accept.

"The Ashland meeting is a reunion of old-time black ballplayers, isn't it?" she asked.

Satchel agreed that it was.

"Well, that's you," she said. "Have you looked in the mirror lately?"

So Satchel passed up the opportunity to meet with the president. As feeble as he was, he made the trip to Kentucky and joined his old friends. As he came before the group, he had plastic tubes in his nose to supplement his oxygen supply. Although he was weak, he pushed away the chair that was offered to him because he wanted to stand to address his fellow Negro leaguers.

"I wasn't the only one who could pitch in the Negro leagues," Satchel reminded them. "We had a lot of Satchels. . . . We had quite a few men who could hit the ball like Babe (Ruth) and Josh (Gibson). . . . They said we couldn't play ball. They said we had tails. But we showed them we're people like anybody else."

The players agreed that the hardships they faced in the Negro leagues taught them how to survive, to fall down and get back up again. Willie Mays, who went on to star in the major leagues, said of his days in the Negro leagues: "They made me survive." He remembered playing for the Birmingham Black Barons as a teenager and being knocked down by a wild pitch. He lay at the plate waiting for help. But none came. Finally his manager walked out and asked, "Can you see first base?" Mays said that he could. "Well

93

get up and get on it," the manager told him and walked back to the dugout.

Satchel thought baseball had become too much of a business to modern players. "I loved baseball. I ate and slept it," he said. "But now players, instead of picking up the sports page, pick up the *Wall Street Journal*."

Satchel continued to weaken and was confined to a wheelchair. Lahoma was with him night and day and watched him deteriorate. Sometimes his shortness of breath and weakening condition went away for a while, then returned.

Still, Satchel kept making personal appearances. On June 5, 1982 Kansas City honored him by dedicating a ballpark and renaming it Satchel Paige Field. John Shuerholz, general manager of the Kansas City Royals, was present for the ceremony and described it as "a positive and moving day." After throwing out the first ball at the dedication, Satchel said, "Nobody on earth could feel as good as I do now."

Three days later Satchel was to be in Louisville, Kentucky, with Bob Feller, but he never arrived. He died of a heart attack on that day, June 8, 1982. After a violent rainstorm, a power failure left his neighborhood with no electricity, and Satchel, who depended on his humidifier and fan, became extremely uncomfortable. He called to his daughter. When she came, she found him in a stupor. Lahoma tried cardiopulmonary resuscitation, but Satchel did not recover and died in the ambulance on the way to the hospital.

Always loved by his fans,
Satchel was honored shortly
before his death in 1982 at
Kansas City where a ballpark
was renamed Satchel Paige Field.

Friends and reporters lavished praise on Satchel. On hearing of his death, John Schuerholz, general manager of the Kansas City Royals, said: "He's a legend in baseball. He did as much as anyone to create an interest in baseball."

Another writer said, "What he achieved in baseball above and beyond the extravagances of his legend, was a career unparalleled in the long history of the game. There was no one like Satchel."

"He was a humble man," Buck O'Neil observed. He recalled hearing Satchel say, "There's something bigger than we are."

"Satchel was truly a presence," Bill Veeck said. "There was an aura of excitement about him."

A *Jet* editor wrote: "No plot on earth could be dug deep enough and wide enough to house the legend that was born 75 years ago in Mobile, Alabama and today lives in the heart and history of baseball fans and sports pages everywhere."

At his funeral, the Reverend Emmanuel Cleaver, the family's pastor for many years, said: "Don't be sad, at least not for Satchel. . . . Satchel Paige has pitched a complete inning. . . . Right now somewhere in glory, God and Satchel are having a big inning."

13

SATCHEL'S IMPACT

Because of racial conditions during his youth, Satchel might well have expected that several opportunities open to white baseball players would never be available to him. Yet, he refused to be bound by the conditions which then existed or to limit his sights to what seemed possible. Satchel overcame numerous obstacles and achieved greater success than most blacks would have dared to dream of when he began his playing career.

None of the barriers to recognition of Satchel's pitching brilliance were overcome by luck. Satchel could never have been considered lucky. Born black in racially segregated Mobile, Alabama, he had five years of reform school on his record by the time he was eighteen. He began his pitching career at a time when most black baseball players struggled to make a decent living. When he reached his prime, the door to the major leagues was still shut tight to blacks, and when the color line was finally broken, Satchel had lost a lot of the speed which had so amazed batters a decade earlier.

But Satchel made doors open. His skill and charisma caused him to be such a gate attraction that at times his salary was four times the major league average. As one reporter put it, "The words 'Satchel Paige to pitch' filled ballparks." Satchel brought excitement to the game. Bill Veeck once said, "If you knew nothing about baseball and you walked into a ballpark, you just knew there was something different about this guy—something that just transmitted itself."

When Satchel began to play baseball professionally, major league ballparks were closed to Negro leaguers. But when other parks could no longer hold the crowds that came to see Satchel and the Crawfords, the gates to the big league parks opened for them.

The extent to which Satchel's pitching was influential in bringing about integration in major league baseball will never be known. He brought out crowds to see blacks play against whites, thus giving many fans, managers, scouts, and sportswriters a chance to see how talented the black players were.

Blacks were admitted to the big leagues too late to give Satchel time to meet the Hall of Fame requirement of ten years in the majors. Yet, because of the widespread recognition that Satchel and other Negro leaguers belonged in the Cooperstown museum, the rules were changed to give them a place there.

Satchel became a national figure and a folk hero. He pitched professionally for forty-three years, and is estimated to have pitched over 2,500 games, more games than anybody in baseball history. It is estimated that he won about 2,000 of them and pitched 300 shutouts and 55 no-hitters.

Satchel showed true pitching genius and the ability to deal with difficult situations through humor. He was aware of his pitching gift and was determined to develop it through practice. In an interview with historian Stephen Banker, Satchel said, "You're born with speed, see, but you can get the control. We had a lot of players when I came up who could throw the ball hard, way harder than I could . . . but they couldn't gain the control. It's such a thing as I practiced all the time. I just practiced control. Anything you practice, you begin to become good at, whether it's baseball or not."

Although Satchel was looked up to by people of all races, he was a particular encouragement to blacks. Donn Rogosin, author of *Invisible Men* said, "Black people, crushed by segregation, desperately needed role models to emulate, and they required men and women who cast large shadows, large enough to make known the truth of black talent."

At a time when blacks were treated unfairly and denied equal rights, yet had no way to speak back, Satchel spoke back for them. He did not make speeches or carry banners, but he outpitched the best white pitchers and struck out the best white batters. For his black fans who were constantly told, "We don't serve niggers here," Satchel spoke back for them by refusing to play in towns where he was not served food or allowed to stay in the hotels. When blacks were denied fair wages, they took pride in knowing that at one time, Satchel Paige was the highest-paid player in baseball. And when they had only a few options open to them, they delighted in the independence he showed when he said: "I'm Satchel. I do as I do."

STATISTICS

SATCHEL'S NEGRO LEAGUE PITCHING CAREER

YEAR(S)	CLUB	LEAGUE
1924–26	Mobile Tigers (semipro)	
1926–27	Chattanooga Black Lookouts	Negro Southern League
1927–29	Birmingham Black Barons	Negro Southern League
1930	Nashville Elite Giants	Negro Southern League
	(Became Cleveland Elite Giants)	
1931–34	Pittsburgh Crawfords	Negro National League
1934–36	Bismarck, N.D. (semipro)	
1936	Pittsburgh Crawfords	Negro National League
1937	Trujillo Stars (Dominican Republic)	
1938	Mexican League	
1939–48	Kansas City Monarchs	Negro American League

In addition to the clubs listed, Satchel pitched for a number of other teams, often on a one-game basis. Altogether he pitched for about 250 teams.

Statistics were rarely kept in the Negro leagues. However, his career in organized baseball is well documented.

SATCHEL'S CAREER IN ORGANIZED BASEBALL

YEAR	CLUB	LEAGUE	G	IP	W	L	Pct	H	R	ER	SO	BB	ERA
1948	Cleveland	American	21	73	6	1	.857	61	21	20	45	25	2.47
1949	Cleveland	American	31	83	4	7	.364	70	29	28	54	33	3.04
1950	barnstorming												
1951	St. Louis	American	23	62	3	4	.429	67	39	33	48	29	4.79
1952	St. Louis	American	46	138	12	10	.545	116	51	47	91	57	3.07
1953	St. Louis	American	57	117	3	9	.250	114	51	46	51	39	3.54
1954–55	barnstorming												
1956	Miami	International	37	111	11	4	.733	101	29	23	79	28	1.86
1957	Miami	International	40	119	10	8	.556	98	35	32	76	11	2.42
1958	Miami	International	28	110	10	10	.500	94	44	36	40	15	2.95
1959–60	barnstorming												
1961	Portland	Pacific Coast	5	25	0	0	.000	28	12	8	19	5	2.88
1962–63–64	barnstorming												
1965	Kansas City	American	1	3	0	0	.000	1	0	0	1	0	0.00
1966	Peninsula	Carolinas	1	2	0	0	.000	5	2	2	0	0	9.00
	Totals			179	483	28	31	.475	429	191	174	290	183	3.88

WORLD SERIES RECORD

YEAR	CLUB	LEAGUE	G	IP	W	L	Pct	H	R	ER	SO	BB	ERA
1948	Cleveland	American	1	2/3	0	0	.000	0	0	0	0	0	0.00

Satchel pitched professionally for forty-three years and is estimated to have pitched over 2,500 games, more games than anyone in history. Experts believe that he won about 2,000 of them and pitched over 300 shutouts and 55 no-hitters.

From 1929 to 1958 he played both summer and winter. He claimed to have once pitched 153 games in a single year.

His best strikeouts-per-game record appears to have been 22, which he achieved several times (including one game against major league barnstormers in 1930).

In his first three starts in the major leagues he drew 201,829 fans and set nighttime attendance records in Chicago and Cleveland.

He was the oldest rookie in major league history. In 1948 he was named Rookie of the Year.

He was appointed to the American League All-Star team in 1952 and 1953.

In 1968 and 1969 he was pitcher-coach for the Atlanta Braves.

He was inducted into the National Baseball Hall of Fame in 1971.

FOR
FURTHER READING

NONFICTION

Frommer, Harvey. *Jackie Robinson*. New York: Franklin Watts, 1984.

Gutman, Bill. *Munsen * Garvey * Brock * Carew*. New York: Grosset & Dunlap, 1976.

Honig, Donald. *Up from the Minor Leagues*. New York: Cowles, 1970.

Libby, Bill. *Baseball's Greatest Sluggers*. New York: Random House, 1973.

Liss, Howard. *Baseball's Zaniest Stars*. New York: Random House, 1971.

Lyttle, Richard B. *A Year in the Minors*. Garden City, New York: Doubleday, 1973.

Reichler, Joseph L. *Fabulous Baseball Facts, Feats and Figures*. New York: Macmillan, 1981.

Robinson, Ray. *Baseball's Most Colorful Managers*. New York: G. P. Putnam's Sons, 1969.

Rubin, Robert. *Lou Gehrig Courageous Star*. New York: G. P. Putnam's Sons, 1979.

Schoor, Gene. *Yogi Berra*. Garden City, New York: Doubleday, 1976.

Young, A. S. "Doc". *The Mets from Mobile, Cleon Jones and Tommie Agee*. New York: Harcourt, Brace & World, 1970.

FICTION

Gault, William Campbell. *Trouble at Second*. New York: E. P. Dutton, 1973.

Higdon, Hal. *The Last Series*. New York: E. P. Dutton, 1974.

Konigsburg, E. L. *Throwing Shadows*. New York: Atheneum, 1979.

Lipsyte, Robert. *Jock and Jill*. New York: Harper & Row, 1982.

Slote, Alfred. *Tony and Me*. New York: J. B. Lippincott, 1974.

INDEX